ITALIAN VEGETARIAN COOKING

ITALIAN

VEGETARIAN COOKING

JO MARCANGELO

Illustrated by Clive Birch

HEALING ARTS PRESS
Rochester, Vermont

Healing Arts Press
One Park Street
Rochester, Vermont 05767

Library of Congress Cataloging-in-Publication Data

Marcangelo, Jo.
  Italian vegetarian cooking / by Jo Marcangelo ; illustrated by
Clive Birch. -- 1st U.S. ed.
    p. cm.
  ISBN 0-89281-343-1 :
  1. Vegetarian cookery. 2. Cookery, Italian. I. Birch, Clive.
II. Title.
TX837.M297 1989
641.5'636--dc20
                                       88-15552
                                           CIP

Printed and bound in the United States

10 9 8 7 6 5 4 3

Healing Arts Press is a division of Inner Traditions International, Ltd.

Distributed to the book trade in Canada by Book Center, Inc., Montreal, Quebec

Distributed to the health food trade in Canada by Alive Books, Toronto and Vancouver

Contents

Introduction

The purpose of this book is to share with you some of my favourite Italian dishes, using fresh vegetables, 100% wholemeal flour and other natural ingredients which are part of the wholefood way of life.

The best cooking in Italy is found in the home. Italian housewives go daily to markets to choose fresh fruit and vegetables: this is time-consuming of course, but they have a high regard for food and take an immense pleasure in shopping for the best quality ingredients and cooking attractive meals for their families. The main meal of the day is taken at lunch time and is an important social occasion for the family. Fathers come home from work and children from school, and there is sufficient time for the whole family to gather around the table to exchange the news and gossip of the day and to share in the enjoyment of mama's cooking. This pattern of eating has been maintained by the custom of shutting down the whole country at midday for two hours or more.

As a guide I have outlined below for you what could be the sequence for a typical vegetarian Italian meal. The first course of an Italian meal usually consists of a *minestra* (soup, pasta dish or risotto), followed by a vegetarian entrée or, perhaps, a selection of cooked seasonal vegetables served with a sauce. If liked, a raw vegetable salad can be served afterwards. To end the meal, there is usually cheese and fresh fruit in season. For special occasions, dinner parties and buffets a simple *antipasto* may be served before the minestra and a dessert before the fruit and cheese. *Minestra*, which is the Italian word for soup, is also used to mean the first course whether it is a soup or not. This is because to the Italians, the first proper course, even when it has been preceded by an *antipasto*, it is still regarded as a soup. Although cakes can be served as a dessert to round off a light meal, Italians would be more likely to serve these with coffee in the morning or midafternoon.

In selecting the recipes I have tried to balance the regional flavours, and an attempt has been made to go beyond the standard recipes that are normally encountered in Italian cookbooks and the more usual dishes to be met within Italian restaurants. Of course, many of the well-known dishes are here but, thanks to family and friends, it has also been possible to include less familiar recipes.

Writing this book has been a delightful and interesting experience, and I hope that those who use it will discover for themselves the pleasures of Italian cooking.

JO MARCANGELO

1. The Italian Store Cupboard

Certain ingredients are frequently used in Italian dishes and it is useful to keep a stock of them handy. The most important are:

Olive oil: Good olive oil is essential. It should have both the colour and taste of the green olives. The quality of the olive, the time of picking and the method used for crushing determines the quality of the oil produced. Cold-pressed olive oil retains all its natural goodness and is very digestable and should be used wherever possible. When buying olive oil look for pure *'extra-vergine'* olive oil on the label of the bottle; good olive oil should look 'murky' with a sign of sediment on the bottom. Olive oil is used in almost every dish in central and southern Italy, though in northern Italy butter may be preferred.

Tomatoes: The tomato is an essential ingredient in many Italian sauces. When fresh tomatoes are expensive, use Italian tinned peeled plum tomatoes. The most widely used plum tomatoes in Italy are called San Marzano. When buying tins look for San Marzano on the label and the words 'imported from Italy'. The tomatoes inside should be a deep, ripe red, firm, and whole, for this shows that they are hand-picked and naturally ripened tomatoes.

Tomato purée: Can be bought in tubes or tins. The former are more useful, since often only a teaspoonful of purée is required, and a tube will keep for a long time after it has been opened.

Vegetable stock A large number of Italian soups and risotti are based on broth or stock. You should always have some home-made vegetable stock on hand. Clear vegetable stock cubes can be used as a short cut and these are available from wholefood shops.

Beans Dried haricot, borlotti and cannellini beans, chick peas (Garbanzo beans) and lentils are used for soups, salads and other dishes.

Pine nuts or pine kernels The nuts which come from the cones of the stone pine are ¼ in. (5mm) long, cream-coloured and slightly oily. They are used in Italy in all kinds of cooking from vegetable dishes to cakes. You can usually buy them at wholefood and health food shops.

Capers These are the small, green, unripe fruit of a plant that grows wild clinging to walls and cliffs, all round the Mediterranean. They make a tangy addition to sauces and may be used on pizzas. You can buy them pickled in brine or vinegar. Some Italian shops sell them packed in salt, and these are much better than the pickled ones. However, they are more perishable too, so only buy from a reliable source where turnover is good.

Olives Black or green olives are used in many dishes. Try to buy them loose from the delicatessen counter; they will be sweeter and juicier and less expensive than those small jars of olives preserved in brine.

Garlic: When buying garlic, choose only firm heads that have thick and meaty cloves and avoid any that look shrivelled. Garlic is credited with a large number of health giving properties. It is, for instance, said to be anti-cholesterol. In Italian cooking it is an indispensable ingredient. For a mild garlic flavour crush a clove, peel off the papery skin, then fry in oil until golden and remove and discard the garlic before using the oil to prepare your sauce. For a stronger flavour chop the garlic clove very finely before frying it and leave it in the sauce. In both cases do not allow the garlic to burn, as this gives a bitter taste. If you are worried about the strong smell of garlic, eat some fresh parsley after your meal. It is an effective antidote.

Pepper and salt: Italians always use freshly ground black pepper from a pepper mill because it is more aromatic. Black pepper is the whole fruit of the pepper plant. Its flavour will fade, so only buy it in small quantities. Sea salt, both fine and coarse, is widely used. Its keener flavour means that you may have to use less to bring out the true taste of the food. Sea salt contains various other elements besides sodium chloride, in a natural balance which helps it to be used efficiently by the body. Like sugar, sodium chloride only becomes a threat to health when it is taken from its natural chemical compound and used in concentrated form, or in large quantities. The latter should not be necessary, since sea salt is used to complement the flavours of Italian food, not to swamp them.

Herbs

Herbs are an essential flavouring in many Italian dishes and, like a regional accent, sometimes give away their place of origin. Whenever possible it is obviously better to use fresh herbs, and it is well worth growing a selection of herbs in pots on the kitchen window-sill or in the garden. Use dried herbs when fresh ones are not available, but they need to be used with care. Replace dried herbs regularly to avoid staleness. The following are most commonly used in Italian cooking:

Parsley *(Prezzemolo)*: The universal herb for flavouring Italian savoury dishes. The Italians use *prezzemolo*, the more pungent flat-leaved variety, sometimes also known as 'continental parsley'. For Italian cooking you should really use this kind of parsley, but if it is not available do not let this worry you.

Sage *(Salvia)*: The grey-green furry leaves of the sage plant makes a lovely scented herb-bread (see recipe for *Focaccia alla salvia* on page 93). If you can grow your own sage or buy it fresh, it is preferable to the dried variety. Whenever possible buy dried whole sage leaves still on the branch, from Italian or Greek grocers.

Bay Leaves *(Lauro)*: Part of the laurel family, the leaves of the bay tree are used in Italian cooking to flavour soups and sauces.

Oregano *(Origano)*: This herb is very popular in Italy, where it grows wild. The leaves are used to flavour soups, sauces and pizzas. Marjoram can be used as a substitute, although its flavour is less strong.

Rosemary *(Rosmarino)*: The grey-green spiky leaves of this fragrant bush are very popular in Italy but must be used with caution as rosemary is a strongly-flavoured herb.

Basil *(Basilico)*: Basil, also known as Sweet Basil, is one of my favourite herbs. It is used a lot in Italy, especially in Genoa, where they say it grows the best. Italians add it to soups, salads, tomato sauces and is used to make *Pesto* (page 126), that wonderful concoction of fresh basil leaves, olive oil, pine nuts and grated Parmesan cheese. Fresh basil should be used whenever possible, but for *Pesto* there is no substitute so I strongly recommend growing it yourself.

Italian Cheeses

Italy produces probably the most widely varied selection of cheese of any country in the world. The listing below should serve to make clearer the characteristics of some of the finest Italian cheeses exported to other countries, and most of the ones mentioned here should be fairly easy to locate in good delicatessens and specialist cheese shops.

Parmesan: is a unique cheese made from skimmed cow's milk and is produced by five small provinces around Parma. It is pale straw-yellow in colour and has a mellow, slightly salty taste. A good Parmesan cheese should be honeycombed with pinpoint holes, finely and closely grained; from this graining comes the name *grana* by which the cheese is commonly known in Italy. Parmesan should be two to three years old, and the more mature it is, the better it tastes. Genuine Parmesan will have the words 'Parmigiano-Reggiano' stencilled on the rind of large pieces, or the labels 'Italian Parmesan' or 'Imported from Italy' on the package and this is what you should look for when buying. For this reason, it is best bought by the piece; packets of ready-grated Parmesan cannot compare with the freshly grated cheese. Parmesan is used a great deal in Italian dishes and its cooking qualities are unique, as it never goes stringy. There is no real substitute, but a mature Cheddar which you have grated yourself is the next best thing.

Pecorino: is a general term for hard, sharp cheeses made from ewe's milk. In many parts of Italy, and especially in country districts, it is often served instead of Parmesan. There are many versions of this cheese throughout Italy, the best known being *Pecorino Romano* and *Pecorino Sardo* from Sardinia.

Fontina: is named after Mount Fontin overlooking Piedmont. It is a very rich, full fat, creamy cheese made from cow's milk. It is ivory in colour and has a firm texture which is occasionally broken by tiny holes. True Fontina, by Italian law, may be made only in the Val d'Aosta region.

Taleggio: originally from the Bergamo area in Lombardy, but now produced elsewhere, is a soft creamy cheese which becomes runny on ripening. It is square and flat with a tender crust and has a slightly aromatic flavour.

Bel Paese: is a fairly recent addition – it was developed in the 1920s by Egidio Galbani. The company he founded now makes it in the U.S.A. and in several other countries under licence, as well as in Italy. It is a semi-soft cheese made from cow's milk. It is a good cheese for cooking, and can often be used as a substitute for Mozzarella, as well as being a popular table cheese.

Gorgonzola: comes from Lombardy. It is made from cow's milk and is a creamy blue-veined cheese, slightly sharp, and one of the best of its type. It is no wonder that it is acclaimed in Italy as *'il Re de Formaggio'* – the King of Cheeses. The curd for gorgonzola is traditionally left until a natural mould starts to form and the cheeses are then turned frequently on racks until the mould has penetrated right through. Copper wires are used to ventilate the cheese nowadays, thus inducing and ensuring speedy growth of mould throughout the curd. When ripe, it should be mild and soft. An excellent table cheese.

Provolone: is made from buffalo's or cow's milk. It comes in various shapes and sizes; a large sausage-shape, pear-shaped and cylindrical. It is a delicate creamy cheese when fresh, with a soft but firm texture. After two or three months the flavour sharpens and develops a piquant taste.

Caciocavallo: is similar to Provolone. It was originally spelled *cacio a cavallo*, which literally translates as 'cheese on horseback', so called because of the way two of them are strung together as if astride a horse.

Mozzarella: or *fior di latte*, as it is properly called when it is not made from buffalo's milk, is a smooth creamy-white cheese which has a very slightly sour tang. It is sold in small quantities and, when very fresh, is moist and dripping with whey. Unless it is in a sealed plastic packet, it is best kept in water to hold in the moisture, and placed in the refrigerator. It is valued in cooking for its melting properties, especially as a topping for pizzas. Bel Paese can be used as a substitute.

Ricotta: is a very white, soft, bland cheese made from whey or buttermilk. As it is very perishable it must be used absolutely fresh. It can be eaten as it is, with honey or fruit, or used in cooking for cheesecakes, gnocchi and as a filling for ravioli, etc. Low-fat curd cheese makes a good substitute.

2. Starters
Antipasti

Italian *antipasti* are very regional, as is all Italian cooking, and vary enormously from the formal approach by northerners to the simple vegetables, sweet peppers and olives of the Sicilian kitchen.

Although some might say that *antipasti* are an integral part of the Italian meal many people dispense with this course nowadays and start with either a rice or spaghetti dish, depending on whether they are from the north or south. The general feeling is that the most appropriate place for *antipasti* is in a restaurant or for formal dinner parties and buffets.

When served at a family meal *antipasti* are likely to consist of fresh vegetables dressed with olive oil and lemon juice or vinegar, as are salads. Sometimes the Italians will serve small pizzas as a starter, or *Bruschetta* (Italian garlic bread). Apart from the recipes in this section many other dishes from the book can be served as starters. It is simply a question of adjusting the quantities.

TOMATO FRITTERS
Bigné di pomodori

(Serves 4)

Imperial (Metric)	American
1 teaspoonful dried yeast, or	1 teaspoonful dried yeast, or
¼oz (7g) fresh yeast	¼ ounce fresh yeast
¼ teaspoonful raw cane sugar	¼ teaspoonful raw cane sugar
¼ pint (150ml) warm milk	⅔ cupful warm milk
4 medium under-ripe tomatoes	4 medium under-ripe tomatoes
½lb (225g) wholemeal flour	2 cupsful wholewheat flour
1 level teaspoonful sea salt	1 level teaspoonful sea salt
1 tablespoonful corn oil	1 tablespoonful corn oil
2 eggs	2 eggs
Vegetable oil for deep-frying	Vegetable oil for deep-drying
To garnish:	*To garnish:*
1 small lemon cut into wedges	1 small lemon cut into wedges
A few sprigs of fresh parsley	A few sprigs of fresh parsley

1. Cream the yeast and sugar with 4 tablespoonsful of the warm milk in a cup or small basin. Leave for 10 minutes to froth up.

2. Place the tomatoes in boiling water for 30 seconds. Remove skins and seeds and chop roughly.

3. Put the flour and salt into a large mixing bowl. Make a well in the centre and pour into it the oil, whole egg and egg yolk. Add the yeast. Whisk together the ingredients, working towards the edges of the bowl. Continue whisking, adding the remainder of the milk a little at a time, until a smooth, thick batter the consistency of whipped cream is obtained. Fold in the pieces of tomato.

4. Whisk the remaining egg white, until stiff but not dry. Gently fold into the batter. Cover and leave in a warm place for about an hour, until doubled in size.

5. Drop half a teaspoonful of the batter into the oil to test the temperature: if it sizzles on contact, the oil is sufficiently hot for frying. A deep-frying thermometer should read 375°F (190°C). Drop tablespoonful of the batter in the oil and cook, a few at a time, for about 3-4 minutes, until puffed up and golden. Drain on crumpled greaseproof paper. Serve the fritters with lemon wedges and sprigs of parsley.

FRIED CHEESE SANDWICHES
Mozzarella in carrozza

(Serves 4)

Imperial (Metric)	American
1 small loaf wholemeal bread	1 small loaf wholewheat bread
½ lb (225 g) fresh Mozzarella cheese	8 ounces fresh Mozzarella cheese
2 eggs	2 eggs
Sea salt and freshly ground black pepper	Sea salt and freshly ground black pepper
Vegetable oil, enough to come at least ¼ in. (5 mm) up the sides of the frying pan	Vegetable oil, enough to come at least ¼ inch up the sides of the frying pan

1. Thinly slice the bread, trim off the crusts. Then slice the Mozzarella cheese, about ¼ in. (5 mm) thick.

2. Make sandwiches in the usual way, using the Mozzarella as a filling. (Allow two thin slices of bread for each person).

3. In a shallow dish, beat the eggs well with a little salt and pepper. Dip the sandwiches, one at a time, in the beaten egg. Press the edges firmly together, so that the cheese is well enclosed.

4. Fry them quickly in hot oil until they are crisp and brown on each side. Drain on kitchen paper and serve while still hot.

Note: If Mozzarella is not available, use Bel Paese or Cheddar cheese for the sandwiches.

ITALIAN GARLIC BREAD
Bruschetta

(Serves 4)

The name *bruschetta* comes from the word *bruscare*, which means 'to roast over coals', the best and most original way of toasting bread. In the districts of Tuscany and Umbria which produce olive oil, the *bruschetta* are eaten with unrefined oil, the first cold virgin pressing of olives which is green, very dense and is rich in flavour.

Imperial (Metric)	American
8 thick slices wholemeal bread, preferably home-made	8 thick slices wholewheat bread, preferably home-made
3-4 cloves of garlic, lightly crushed with a heavy knife-handle and peeled	3.4 cloves of garlic, lightly crushed with a heavy knife-handle and peeled
Approx. 3 fl oz (90ml) olive oil, as green and dense as you can find	Approx. ⅓ cupful olive oil, as green and dense as you can find

1. Preheat the grill.
2. Toast the bread on both sides until crisp and golden-brown.
3. Rub one side of the toast with garlic while still hot. Discard the garlic as it dries up and take a fresh clove. Arrange the pieces of toast on four warm plates with the garlic-rubbed side upwards, and pour a thin stream of olive oil over it – not just a few drops, but enough to soak each slice very lightly. (You can regulate the flow by pouring the oil from a bottle with a cork in which a groove has been cut). Serve at once.

OLIVE PASTE
Crema di oliva

(Makes about 1 pound/450g)

Imperial (Metric)	American
1 lb (450g) black olives, stoned	4 cupsful black olives, stoned
1 clove of garlic, peeled (optional)	1 clove of garlic, peeled (optional)
3 fl oz (90 ml) olive oil, preferably 'extra-virgin'	1/3 cupful olive oil, preferably 'extra-virgin'
1 tablespoonful oregano	1 tablespoonful oregano
Sea salt	Sea salt

1. Place all the ingredients in a blender or food processor. The machine will have to be stopped frequently and a rubber spatula used to push the mixture onto the blender blades repeatedly until a smooth paste is obtained.

2. Taste and adjust seasoning. Put in tightly covered glass jars and label with date.

Note: Crema di oliva may be used as a sauce on all types of pasta, spread on toast and eaten as a starter, or used as an accompaniment with hard-boiled eggs and vegetables.

— olive paste —

SICILIAN SWEET AND SOUR VEGETABLES
Caponata

(Serves 4)

Imperial (Metric)	American
3 large aubergines	3 large eggplants
Sea salt	Sea salt
5 celery sticks	5 celery stalks
3 fl oz (90 ml) olive oil	⅓ cupful olive oil
1 large onion, chopped	1 large onion, chopped
1 lb (450g) fresh ripe tomatoes, blanched, seeded and chopped *or*	1 pound fresh ripe tomatoes, blanched, seeded and chopped *or*
14 oz (400g) tin tomatoes, well drained and chopped	1 medium can tomatoes, well drained and chopped
2 tablespoonsful tomato purée	2 tablespoonsful tomato paste
2 teaspoonsful raw cane sugar	2 teaspoonsful raw cane sugar
3 tablespoonsful capers, rinsed	3 tablespoonsful capers, rinsed
4 oz (100g) green olives, stoned	1 cupful green olives, stoned
3 tablespoonsful wine vinegar	3 tablespoonsful wine vinegar
2 tablespoonsful fresh parsley, chopped	2 tablespoonsful fresh parsley, chopped

1. Wipe the aubergines (eggplants) and cut them into ½ inch (1 cm) cubes. Put them into a colander, sprinkle generously with salt. Let them stand for about 1 hour, during which time the salt will draw out any bitterness along with excess moisture. After that, rinse and pat dry with kitchen paper.

2. Cut the celery into ½ inch (1 cm) cubes. Cook in boiling salted water for about 5-7 minutes. Drain well.

3. Heat 4 tablespoonsful of the oil in a large frying pan over moderate heat. Add the aubergine (eggplant) and fry to a pale-golden colour, stirring frequently to prevent them from soaking too much oil. Remove from the pan and drain on kitchen paper.

4. Heat the remaining oil in a large, heavy-based saucepan, add the onion and celery and fry until almost tender. Remove from the pan.

5. In the same pan, add the tomatoes, tomato purée, sugar and a little salt and pepper. Cook gently, uncovered, for about 5 minutes. Stir in the aubergine (eggplant), capers, onion, celery, olives and the

vinegar. Simmer for a few minutes, stirring occasionally. Taste and check the seasoning. Remove from the heat and allow to cool. Serve chilled in individual dishes, sprinkled with chopped parsley.

Note: It is necessary to prepare this dish in advance so that the flavours are absorbed by the vegetables.

STUFFED EGGS WITH CHEESE
Uova farcite con formaggio

(Serves 6)

Imperial (Metric)	American
6 hard-boiled eggs, shelled	6 hard-boiled eggs, shelled
3oz (75g) Gorgonzola or blue cheese	¾ cupful Gorgonzola or blue cheese
3-4 tablespoonsful soured cream	3-4 tablespoonsful sour cream
1 teaspoonful cider vinegar or lemon juice	1 teaspoonful cider vinegar or lemon juice
Lettuce	Lettuce
2-3 sprigs fresh parsley	2-3 sprigs fresh parsley

1. Cut the hard-boiled eggs in half lengthwise and remove the yolks carefully.

2. Combine the egg yolks with the cheese, soured cream and vinegar or lemon juice. Mix well.

3. Fill egg whites with the mixture and place on a bed of lettuce. Garnish each half with a fresh parsley leaf.

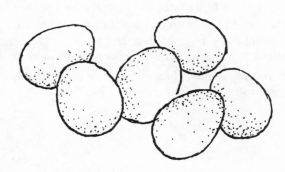

BREADSTICKS
Grissini

(Makes about 16)

This is a wholemeal version of the famous Italian breadsticks. They originated from the city of Turin in the north of Italy.

Imperial (Metric)	American
¼ oz (7g) fresh yeast or	1½ teaspoonsful fresh yeast or
1 teaspoonful dried yeast	1 teaspoonful dried yeast
1 teaspoonful honey	1 teaspoonful honey
⅓ pint (200ml) warm water	¾ cupful warm water
½ lb (225g) wholemeal flour	2 cupsful wholewheat flour
1 teaspoonful sea salt	1 teaspoonful sea salt
1 tablespoonful olive oil	1 tablespoonful olive oil
1 egg, well beaten	1 egg, well beaten
2 tablespoonsful sesame seeds	2 tablespoonsful sesame seeds

1. Mix the yeast, honey and 3-4 tablespoonsful of the warm water, and set aside for 5 or 10 minutes, or until mixture is frothy.

2. Put the flour and salt into a warm bowl, make a well in the centre, and pour in the yeast mixture, then the oil and enough of the remaining warm water to make a pliable dough. Turn out and knead for 3 or 4 minutes, until smooth and elastic.

3. Cover with a damp tea towel and leave in a warm place until doubled in size, about 1 hour. Knock down and knead again until smooth.

4. Divide the dough into 16 equal pieces and roll them with the palm of your hands into sticks about the width of your finger. Place them on an oiled baking sheet.

5. Brush them with beaten egg and sprinkle with sesame seeds.

6. Bake the sticks in an oven preheated to 400°F/200°C (Gas Mark 6) for 20-25 minutes, or until they are golden-brown. Transfer the breadsticks to a wire rack to cool; serve them warm or cold.

Variations: You can sprinkle breadsticks with poppy or caraway seeds or coarse sea salt before baking.

STUFFED MUSHROOMS WITH SPINACH AND BECHAMEL SAUCE
Funghi ripieni con spinaci e salsa balsamella

(Serves 4)

Imperial (Metric)	American
8 large flat mushrooms	8 large flat mushrooms
¾ lb (350g) fresh spinach	12 ounces fresh spinach
2 tablespoonsful olive oil	2 tablespoonsful olive oil
1 small onion, finely chopped	1 small onion, finely chopped
1 clove of garlic, peeled and crushed	1 clove of garlic, peeled and crushed
½ pint (275ml) *Salsa balsamella* medium-thick (page 124)	1⅓ cupsful *Salsa balsamella* medium-thick (page 124)
1 oz (25g) grated Parmesan cheese	¼ cupful grated Parmesan cheese
1 oz (25g) fresh wholemeal breadcrumbs	½ cupful fresh wholewheat breadcrumbs
Sea salt and freshly ground black pepper	Sea salt and freshly ground black pepper

1. Wipe mushrooms, remove stalks; chops stalks finely.

2. Wash spinach, discard any coarse stalks or discoloured leaves. Place it in a heavy-based saucepan with only the water that clings to it. Cover and cook for 7 minutes. Drain the spinach well, pressing out any excess moisture, and chop roughly.

3. Heat the oil in a frying pan, add the onion, garlic and chopped mushroom stalks and fry for 5 minutes. Add the chopped spinach and cook for 2 minutes more.

4. Transfer the contents of the frying pan to a mixing bowl, add 2-3 tablespoonsful of breadcrumbs, the béchamel sauce, grated Parmesan cheese and salt and pepper to taste. Mix well.

5. Arrange the mushroom caps, hollow side up, in an oiled shallow ovenproof dish. Fill with the stuffing and sprinkle with the remaining breadcrumbs. Bake in a fairly hot oven preheated to 375°F/190°C (Gas Mark 5) for 25-30 minutes. Allow to settle for a few minutes before serving.

3. Soups
Minestre

Soups are very popular in Italy. Although 'minestrone' is the name that springs to mind in connection with Italian soups, there is in fact a large variety, some so substantial that they are more like thick stews than anything else. My favourites are the rustic peasant soups, which are very thick vegetable soups with the addition of pulses – haricot (navy) beans or lentils, perhaps – pasta or rice. All regions have their own specialities. In Genoa they add their famous Pesto sauce (page 126) to Minestrone (page 28). The recipes also differ widely from home to home and the ingredients used often consist of what is available. Served with plenty of freshly grated Parmesan cheese, they are not only delicious but also very nourishing.

POTATO AND TOMATO SOUP
Minestra rossa di patate

(Serves 4)

Imperial (Metric)	American
3 large potatoes	3 large potatoes
3 tablespoonsful olive oil	3 tablespoonsful olive oil
½ teaspoonful dried basil or 2-3 fresh leaves, if available	½ teaspoonsful dried basil or 2-3 fresh leaves, if available
2 pints (1.15 litres) vegetable stock or 2 stock cubes dissolved in the same quantity of water	5 cupsful vegetable stock or 2 bouillon cubes dissolved in the same quantity of water
14 oz (400g) tin tomatoes, coarsely chopped	1 medium can tomatoes, coarsely chopped
Sea salt and freshly ground black pepper	Sea salt and freshly ground black pepper
3-4 thick slices wholemeal bread	3-4 thick slices wholewheat bread
Vegetable oil	Vegetable oil
Grated Parmesan cheese	Grated Parmesan cheese

1. Peel potatoes and cut into small cubes.

2. Put the potatoes into a saucepan with the oil, basil, stock and the tomatoes with their juice. Add seasoning to taste.

3. Bring to the boil. Cover, and simmer gently over low heat for 45 minutes to 1 hour, stirring from time to time.

4. Pass the soup through a metal sieve or blend to a smooth purée in an electric liquidizer, then reheat gently. Ladle the soup into individual soup bowls top with *crostini* or croûtons and serve with grated Parmesan cheese separately.

5. *To make the crostini or croûtons:* Remove the crusts from the bread. Cut each slice into fingers and cut across to make cubes. Heat enough oil to come ½ in. (1 cm) up the side of a large frying pan. When the oil is hot, add the cubes in a single layer, lower heat and fry the cubes gently so that they become crisp. To ensure even cooking toss them frequently. Transfer to absorbent paper to drain.

CABBAGE SOUP
Zuppa di cavolo

(Serves 4)

Imperial (Metric)	American
½ lb (225g) dried borlotti beans, soaked overnight and drained	1 cupful dried borlotti beans, soaked overnight and drained
2 tablespoonsful olive oil	2 tablespoonsful olive oil
1 large onion, finely chopped	1 large onion, finely chopped
2 large carrots, finely chopped	2 large carrots, finely chopped
2 celery sticks, finely chopped	2 celery stalks, finely chopped
2 tinned tomatoes, coarsely chopped	2 peeled plum tomatoes, coarsely chopped
¾ lb (350g) white cabbage, finely chopped	3 cupsful finely shredded white cabbage
Sea salt and freshly ground black pepper	Sea salt and freshly ground black pepper
2 tablespoonsful chopped fresh parsley	2 tablespoonsful chopped fresh parsley
4 thick slices wholemeal bread, preferably home-made	4 thick slices wholewheat bread, preferably home-made

1. Place the beans into a large heavy-based saucepan and cover them with at least twice their volume of fresh water. Bring the beans to the boil slowly, then reduce the heat so that they simmer. Cover them with a lid, and cook the beans for about 1½-2 hours, until they feel tender when pressed.

2. In a separate saucepan, heat the oil over a low heat, then add the chopped onion, celery, carrots, tomatoes and the cabbage. Season with salt and pepper to taste. Cover the pan with a tight-fitting lid, and let the vegetables cook in their own juices, undisturbed, for about 15 minutes.

3. When the beans are tender, scoop out about two thirds of the beans with a slotted spoon and put them in a wire sieve over the pan. Use a wooden pestle to press the beans back into the pan, moistening them with some of the liquid to make sieving easier.

4. Add the vegetables to the pan containing the beans, and simmer, uncovered, for a further 30 minutes, by which time the soup will have thickened slightly. Check the seasoning and stir in the chopped parsley.

5. Arrange the toasted bread into four warm soup plates and ladle the soup over.

MINESTRONE SOUP WITH RICE
Minestrone con riso

(Serves 4 to 6)

Imperial (Metric)	American
1 oz (25g) butter or polyunsaturated margarine	2½ tablespoonsful butter or polyunsaturated margarine
1 tablespoonful olive oil	1 tablespoonful olive oil
1 clove of garlic, peeled and crushed	1 clove of garlic, peeled and crushed
1 medium onion, chopped	1 medium onion, chopped
2 celery sticks, chopped	2 celery stalks, chopped
2 large carrots, finely chopped	2 large carrots, finely chopped
½ lb (225g) tin tomatoes, coarsely chopped	1 small can tomatoes, coarsely chopped
2 leeks, sliced	2 leeks, sliced
¼ medium green cabbage, shredded	¼ medium green cabbage, shredded
½ lb (225g) short grain brown rice	1 cupful short grain brown rice
2¾ pints (1.5 litres) vegetable stock or water	7 cupsful vegetable stock or water
Sea salt and freshly ground black pepper	Sea salt and freshly ground black pepper
1 oz (25g) grated Pecorino or Parmesan cheese	¼ cupful grated Pecorino or Parmesan cheese

1. Heat the butter and the oil in a heavy-based saucepan, add the garlic, onion, celery and carrots. Stir in the tomatoes with their juice. Cover and cook over low heat for 10 minutes or so to allow the vegetables to sweat, stirring occasionally.

2. Add the leeks, cabbage and rice. Pour in the vegetable stock or water and bring to the boil. Lower the heat and simmer gently for 45 minutes or until the rice is tender. Check seasoning.

3. Serve in warmed soup bowls, sprinkled with the grated cheese.

GENOESE MINESTRONE
Minestra Genovese

(Serves 8 to 10)

Imperial (Metric)	American
2 fl oz (60 ml) olive oil	1/4 cupful olive oil
2 medium onions, finely sliced	2 medium onions, finely sliced
2 leeks, washed and cut into thin rounds	2 leeks, washed and cut into thin rounds
1 clove of garlic, peeled and crushed	1 clove of garlic, peeled and crushed
2 carrots, finely diced	2 carrots, finely diced
2 celery sticks, finely chopped	2 celery stalks, finely chopped
2 medium potatoes, peeled and diced	2 medium potatoes, peeled and diced
1/2 lb (225 g) courgettes, washed and diced	8 ounces zucchini, washed and diced
1/2 lb (225 g) French beans, cut into 1 inch (2.5 cm) lengths	8 ounces snap beans, cut into 1 inch lengths
1/2 lb (225 g) cabbage, shredded	2 cupsful shredded cabbage
1/2 lb (225 g) tin tomatoes	1 small can tomatoes
6 oz (175 g) fresh peas, shelled weight	1 cupful fresh peas, shelled weight
Rind from a piece of Parmesan cheese (optional)	Rind from a piece of Parmesan cheese (optional)
3 pints (1.7 litres) vegetable stock or water (approx.)	7 1/2 cupsful vegetable stock or water (approx.)
Sea salt and freshly ground black pepper	Sea salt and freshly ground black pepper
14 oz (400 g) tin haricot beans	1 medium can navy beans
6 oz (175 g) wholemeal spaghetti or tagliatelle, broken into 1 inch (2.5 cm) lengths	2 cupsful wholewheat spaghetti or tagliatelle, broken into 1 inch lengths
3 tablespoonsful Pesto Sauce (page 126)	3 tablespoonsful Pesto Sauce (page 126)
2 oz (50 g) freshly grated Parmesan cheese	1/2 cupful freshly grated Parmesan cheese

1. Heat the oil in a large saucepan. Add the onions, leeks and garlic
    and fry gently until they just begin to colour. Add the carrots and
    cook for 2-3 minutes, stirring occasionally. Proceed as above, with
    the celery, potatoes, courgettes (zucchini) and French (snap) beans,
    cooking each one a few minutes and stirring. Add the shredded
    cabbage and cook for about 5 minutes, stirring from time to time.

2. Add the tomatoes and their juice, the peas, the cheese rind (if used),
    and then the stock. Bring to the boil. Season, cover the pan and
    simmer for at least 2 hours.

3. Then add the haricot (navy) beans with their liquid. Bring back to the
    boil, and add the pasta and cook for about 15 minutes until the pasta
    is tender, stirring occasionally. Check the seasoning. Remove the
    pan from the heat, add the Pesto and serve with the grated Parmesan
    cheese passed around separately.

CLIVE BIRCH

RICE AND CHESTNUT SOUP
Minestra di riso e castagne

(Serves 4 to 6)

Imperial (Metric)	American
1 lb (450g) fresh chestnuts	1 pound fresh chestnuts
Sea salt	Sea salt
2 tablespoonsful olive oil	2 tablespoonsful olive oil
1 large onion, finely chopped	1 large onion, finely chopped
1 celery stick, finely chopped	1 celery stalk, finely chopped
1 large carrot, finely chopped	1 large carrot, finely chopped
2¾ pints (1.5 litres) vegetable stock or water	7 cupsful vegetable stock or water
½ lb short grain brown rice	1 cupful short grain brown rice
Freshly ground black pepper	Freshly ground black pepper

1. Wash the chestnuts and make a slit in their skins with a sharp knife (this helps loosen both the shell and the inside skin while the chestnuts boil and makes peeling them easier). Put into a saucepan with enough cold water to cover and a pinch of salt. Bring to the boil, and cook for 25-30 minutes. Drain. Peel the chestnuts while they are still warm.

2. Put the chestnuts through a mouli-légumes using the largest holes available. Alternatively, chop the chestnuts coarsely.

3. Heat the oil in a large saucepan, add the onion, celery and carrot and fry gently for about 10 minutes, stirring frequently. Next, add the chestnuts, the stock or water and bring to the boil.

4. Add the rice, cover and simmer very gently for about 40 minutes, or until the rice is tender but *al dente* (firm to the bite). Stir from time to time to prevent the soup from sticking to the pan. The consistency of the soup should be rather dense. Check the seasoning and ladle into individual soup bowls.

LENTIL SOUP
Zuppa di lenticchie

(Serves 4)

Imperial (Metric)	American
2 tablespoonsful olive oil	2 tablespoonsful olive oil
1 large onion, finely chopped	1 large onion, finely chopped
2 celery sticks, finely chopped	2 celery stalks, finely chopped
2 medium carrots, finely chopped	2 medium carrots, finely chopped
1 clove of garlic, peeled and crushed	1 clove of garlic, peeled and crushed
½ lb (225 g) green or brown whole lentils, washed and drained	1 cupful green or brown whole lentils, washed and drained
½ lb (225 g) tin tomatoes, coarsely chopped, with their juice	1 small can tomatoes, coarsely chopped with their juice
About 2 pints (1.15 litres) vegetable stock	About 5 cupsful vegetable stock
Sea salt and freshly ground black pepper	Sea salt and freshly ground black pepper
Freshly grated Parmesan cheese	Freshly grated Parmesan cheese

1. Heat the oil in a large saucepan and fry the onion until lightly browned. Add the celery, carrots and garlic and fry for a further 2-3 minutes, stirring from time to time.

2. Stir in the lentils, the tomatoes with their juice and the stock. Cover the pan and bring to the boil. Reduce the heat and simmer, stirring occasionally for 45-60 minutes, or until the lentils have cooked and have thickened the soup.

3. Taste the soup for seasoning. Serve in soup bowls with freshly grated Parmesan, passed separately.

Variation: About 10 minutes before the end of the cooking time add 6oz/175g (1½ cupsful) wholemeal 'elbow' macaroni. Adding extra boiling water to the soup, if necessary.

SPLIT GREEN PEA SOUP
Zuppa di piselli secchi

(Serves 6)

Imperial (Metric)	American
About 4 pints (2.25 litres) vegetable stock	About 10 cupsful vegetable stock
1 lb (450g) split green peas, washed and drained	2 cupsful split green peas, washed and drained
2 tablespoonsful olive oil	2 tablespoonsful olive oil
1 large onion, finely chopped	1 large onion, finely chopped
1 celery stick, finely chopped	1 celery stalk, finely chopped
1 large carrot, finely chopped	1 large carrot, finely chopped
Sea salt and freshly ground black pepper	Sea salt and freshly ground black pepper

1. Bring the stock to the boil, add the split peas, cover and simmer over low heat for about 30 minutes.

2. In a second pan, heat the oil, add the chopped onion, celery and carrot and cook covered for about 15 minutes, until the vegetables have softened.

3. Add the softened vegetables to the stock and split peas, season with salt and freshly ground black pepper, cover and simmer gently for a further 45-60 minutes. Stir occasionally to prevent the soup from sticking to the pan.

4. Purée the soup by pressing through a metal sieve or liquidize in an electric blender. Return to the saucepan and bring slowly to the boil. If the soup seems too thick, thin down with extra boiling water; if too thin, boil uncovered until correct consistency is obtained. Taste soup and adjust seasoning. Ladle into warmed soup plates, and serve with *crostini* or croûtons (see page 25).

RICE AND PEAS
Risi e bisi

(Serves 4)

This very thick soup, almost a risotto, is a speciality from Venice.

Imperial (Metric)
2 pints (1.15 litres) vegetable stock
1½ oz (40g) butter or polyunsaturated margarine
1 large onion, finely chopped
2 lbs (900g) fresh peas (unshelled weight)
¾ lb (350g) short grain brown rice
Sea salt, if necessary
2 oz (50g) freshly grated Parmesan

American
5 cupsful vegetable stock
3 tablespoonsful butter or polyunsaturated margarine
1 large onion, finely chopped
2 pounds fresh peas (unshelled weight)
1½ cupsful short grain brown rice
Sea salt, if necessary
½ cupful freshly grated Parmesan

1. Bring the stock slowly to the boil and keep it barely simmering over a low heat.

2. Melt the butter in a heavy-based saucepan, add the onion and fry over a moderate heat until soft, but not browned.

3. Add the shelled peas and the rice, and when the grains of rice become translucent – about 3 minutes – pour in the hot stock. Cover, and simmer over the lowest possible heat for about 40 minutes, or until the rice is tender but *al dente*, firm to the bite. Stirring occasionally, being careful not to break the peas. Check the seasoning.

4. When the rice is cooked, take the pan off the heat, add half of the Parmesan, and serve the rest of the cheese separately.

NEAPOLITAN PASTA AND BEAN SOUP
Pasta e fagioli Napoletana

(Serves 4)

Imperial (Metric)	American
½ lb (225g) dried borlotti beans, soaked overnight and drained	1 cupful dried borlotti beans, soaked overnight and drained
3 pints (1.7 litres) water (approx.)	7½ cupsful water (approx.)
1 onion, finely chopped	1 onion, finely chopped
1 carrot, finely chopped	1 carrot, finely chopped
1 celery stick, finely chopped	1 celery stalk, finely chopped
3 tablespoonsful olive oil	3 tablespoonsful olive oil
1 clove of garlic, peeled and crushed	1 clove of garlic, peeled and crushed
2 tablespoonsful chopped fresh parsley	2 tablespoonsful chopped fresh parsley
½ lb (225g) tin tomatoes	1 small can tomatoes
Sea salt and freshly ground black pepper	Sea salt and freshly ground black pepper
6 oz (175g) wholemeal 'elbow' macaroni	1½ cupsful wholewheat 'elbow' macaroni

1. Put the beans into a heavy-based saucepan with fresh, cold water. Add the chopped onion, carrot, celery and bring to the boil. Cover and simmer for about 2 hours or until the beans are tender.

2. About 30 minutes before the end of the cooking time: heat the oil in a small saucepan, add the garlic and parsley and fry gently for 2 minutes, stirring frequently.

3. Sieve tomatoes and juice and add to the pan with seasoning to taste, and bring to the boil. Cover and simmer gently for 10 minutes, then add to the beans. Let the tomatoes cook with the beans and vegetables for 15 minutes, stirring occasionally.

4. Scoop out about 1 cupful of the beans and purée in a blender or press through a sieve, then return them to the soup.

5. Bring back to the boil, add the pasta and cook until the pasta is tender – about 15 minutes. Stir occasionally to prevent sticking. Taste and adjust the seasoning before serving. If liked, serve with grated Parmesan cheese passed separately.

Note: This soup should be very thick. You may have to cook it uncovered if there is too much liquid, or add a little more stock or water if it has all evaporated during cooking.

BEAN SOUP WITH GARLIC AND PARSLEY
Zuppa di cannellini con aglio e prezzemolo

(Serves 4)

This is a bean-lover's soup, nearly all beans with a little liquid and a hint of garlic.

Imperial (Metric)	American
1 lb (450g) dried cannellini beans, or other white beans, soaked overnight	2⅔ cupful dried white kidney beans, or other white beans, soaked overnight
1 bay leaf	1 bay leaf
Sea salt	Sea salt
3 fl oz (90ml) olive oil	⅓ cupful olive oil
1 clove of garlic	1 clove of garlic
1 oz (25g) fresh parsley, chopped	½ cupful chopped fresh parsley
Freshly ground black pepper	Freshly ground black pepper
1 tablespoonful cider vinegar (optional)	1 tablespoonful cider vinegar (optional)
4 slices wholemeal bread, toasted	4 slices wholewheat bread, toasted

1. Rinse and drain the beans, put them in a large saucepan with the bay leaf and cover with cold water. Bring to the boil and simmer gently, covered, for about 1½-2 hours or until the beans are tender. Salt the beans to taste towards the end of cooking.

2. Drain the beans and reserve ¾ pint/425ml (2 cupsful) of the cooking liquid.

3. Heat the oil in a large saucepan, fry the garlic until just lightly coloured. Add the parsley, beans and the reserved bean liquid. Simmer for a few minutes.

4. Season with salt and a few twists of freshly ground black pepper and the cider vinegar, if used. Serve over slices of toasted wholemeal bread.

4. Pasta

There are many conflicting theories about the origins of pasta in Italy and in other parts of the world. One indisputable fact, however, is that the pasta we know today is the one the Italians have used for the last three centuries. It was in Italy that pasta gained a foothold, but its popularity has grown to make it an internationally accepted food far from Italy's shores.

The Italians, like much of the rest of the world, are getting more conscious of their weight and their health in general. They may still eat platefuls of *pasta asciutta* (a cooked pasta dish with a sauce) but whole meal pasta or *pasta integrale* as it is known in Italy, with its beneficial dietary fibre, is now being recognized by many Italians as an essential part of everyday healthy living. Wholemeal spaghetti, known as *bigoli* by the Venetians, is a very popular choice.

Wholemeal pasta is available in an ever increasing range of sizes, shapes and textures. The best quality is made from pure durum wheat wholemeal flour, without any artificial colouring or preservatives. By law it is permissible for manufacturers to add only natural ingredients such as green vegetables or tomatoes to colour the pasta, and they do not really alter the taste. *Pasta verdi* (green pasta) made with spinach is widely available and, like wholemeal pasta, is obtainable from health food and wholefood shops, and now the more discriminating supermarkets are also stocking it.

I have tried to provide a variety of regional dishes using traditional pasta shapes and ingredients. An average serving of fresh pasta per person would be 2-4 ounces (50-100g) for a starter and 4-5 ounces (100-150g) for a main course. Use a little less dried pasta, as it will swell more when cooked.

The cooking times for bought pasta varies according to the pasta's size, shape and brand, therefore tasting is the only reliable way of testing. The Italian expression for perfectly cooked pasta is *al dente* which literally translated means 'to the tooth' – just tender but still firm to the bite.

Here are some very simple rules for cooking pasta:

- Use 7 pints (4 litres) of water to every 1 pound (450g) of pasta.
- Add salt when the water comes to a boil – about 1½-2 tablespoonsful for every 1 pound (450g) of pasta.
- Add the pasta all at once when the water is at a rolling boil. Never break up long pasta such as spaghetti; simply ease it into the pan as it softens. (A few drops of olive oil added to the water will help to keep the strands separate.)
- Turn up the heat immediately to bring the water back to the boil.
- Cook uncovered.
- Stir occasionally to keep the pasta distributed in the boiling water so it will cook evenly.
- Test frequently to avoid overcooking, as pasta continues to soften until you eat it.

The instant it is done, tip the pasta into a colander, shaking it lightly to remove most of the water. Once the pasta is drained it must be *condita* or 'sauced' quickly, because if you let the pasta stand without coating it will stick together. Turn into a preheated serving dish or individual plates. The 'sauce' can be taken to be a knob of butter, olive oil, Parmasan cheese or a cooked sauce according to the recipe used; whether extra 'sauce' is served separately or tossed in with the pasta is a matter of taste.

The rules for cooking home-made egg pasta are the same, except that it cooks in a fraction of the time – 2 or 3 minutes as opposed to 15 – and when ready will rise to the surface.

HOME-MADE EGG PASTA
Pasta all'uovo

Imperial (Metric)	American
½ lb (225g) 81 or 100% plain wholemeal flour	2 cupsful 81 or 100% plain wholewheat flour
2 eggs	2 eggs
2 teaspoonsful olive oil	2 teaspoonsful olive oil
Pinch of sea salt	Pinch of sea salt
A little water	A little water

1. Place the flour in a large mixing bowl, or in a mound on a clean working surface, and make a well in the centre. (If using 100% wholemeal flour, sift to remove the coarsest particles of bran to make the dough easier to handle. Use the bran in soups, sauces or on cereal.)

2. Put the eggs, oil and salt into the well. Start mixing in the eggs with a fork, drawing in the flour from the inside wall of the well. When the egg mixture is no longer liquid, mix in the rest of the flour with fingertips. Add a few drops of water to moisten any dry areas: taking care not to overwet the dough – it should be fairly firm and dry. (The exact amount of water used depends on the absorbency of the flour and the size of eggs used).

3. Turn out onto a lightly floured surface and knead the dough until it is smooth and elastic – about 15 minutes.

4. Shape into a ball, cover with a damp cloth or a bowl and allow to rest for at least 30 minutes. This will help relax the gluten and make the dough easier to stretch.

5. *To roll:* Divide the dough in half to make it easier to handle. (Keep the rest of the dough covered with a bowl or damp cloth until ready to roll out, or refrigerate in a plastic bag.) Roll out on a lightly floured surface, first in one direction and then in the other, to form a rectangle. As the dough becomes thinner you may need to cut it in half to make the rolling easier. Make sure there are no holes or creases and continue until the dough is paper thin – this takes practice! When the dough is almost translucent, it is thin enough to cut into shapes and used as required. Cover with a clean damp cloth and repeat with the other half of the dough.

6. *To shape:* For simple tagliatelle or fettuccine, dust the pasta sheets with flour and leave to dry for 10-15 minutes, but do not allow to become brittle. Then roll up from the shortest edge to form a loose 'Swiss-roll'. Take a sharp knife and cut the roll into thin slices: ½ in. (1 cm) for tagliatelle and about ¼ in. (5 mm) for fettuccine. Take care not to press down on the roll whilst cutting it or the layers of dough will stick together. Carefully unroll each strip of dough and lay out flat on a tea towel or hang up to dry for 10-15 minutes before cooking. (I find that a clean broomstick suspended between two chairs is ideal for drying the pasta strips).

Note: Pasta dough can also be made successfully in a food processor.

GREEN PASTA
Pasta verde

Follow the same recipe, adding 2 ounces (50g) cooked, very finely chopped spinach (weighed after having been squeezed very dry) to the eggs and flour. You will have to add a little more flour to absorb the spinach. This pasta is softer than plain pasta and frequent flouring of the work surface may be necessary.

LASAGNE WITH PESTO
Lasagne con pesto

(Serves 4)

Imperial (Metric)	American
1 quantity of home-made pasta (page 38)	1 quantity of home-made pasta (page 38)
Sea salt	Sea salt
1 quantity of Pesto Sauce (page 126)	1 quantity of Pesto Sauce (page 126)
1½ oz (40g) butter	3 tablespoonsful butter
1 oz (25g) grated Parmesan cheese	¼ cupful grated Parmesan cheese

1. Roll out the dough as directed on page 39 until it is as thin as you can make it. Cut it into strips about 3 inches (7.5cm) wide and 10 inches (25cm) long.

2. Bring a large pan of salted water to the boil. Cook 3 or 4 sheets at a time very briefly (for about 30 seconds). Remove the lasagne from the pan with a slotted spoon and plunge into a large bowl of cold water in order to stop the cooking. Place the lasagne sheets on a clean towel to drain. Continue with the remaining sheets in the same way, draining as above.

3. Butter a shallow rectangular, ovenproof dish and cover the bottom with a layer of the lasagne. Spread with a thin layer of the Pesto. Repeat these layers, ending with a layer of Pesto Sauce.

4. Dot with the remaining butter, sprinkle over the Parmesan cheese and bake in a preheated oven at 375°F/190°C (Gas Mark 5) for about 20 minutes. Allow the dish to settle for a few minutes before serving.

PASTA SPIRALS WITH CARROTS
Fusilli alle carote

(Serves 4)

Imperial (Metric)	American
2 tablespoonsful olive oil	2 tablespoonsful olive oil
1 small onion, finely chopped	1 small onion, finely chopped
2 cloves of garlic, peeled and crushed	2 cloves of garlic, peeled and crushed
1 celery stick, finely chopped	1 celery stalk, finely chopped
½ lb (225g) carrots, finely grated	1¼ cupsful finely grated carrots
2 tablespoonsful chopped fresh parsley	2 tablespoonsful chopped fresh parsley
½ lb (225g) tin tomatoes	1 small can tomatoes
½ vegetable stock cube	½ vegetable bouillon cube
Sea salt and freshly ground black pepper	Sea salt and freshly ground black pepper
1 lb (450g) wholemeal pasta spirals, or any other pasta shape of your choice	1 pound wholewheat pasta spirals, or any other pasta shape of your choice

1. Heat the oil in a saucepan and fry the onion until transparent. Add the garlic, celery, carrots and parsley. Stir for a few minutes.

2. Add the tomatoes with their juice. Crumble in the stock cube and pour in ¼ pint/150ml (⅔ cupful) of boiling water. Season with salt and a few twists of freshly ground black pepper. Cover and simmer over low heat for 30 minutes.

3. Meanwhile cook the pasta *al dente*. Drain and put in a warmed serving dish. Pour over the sauce and mix well. Serve immediately.

Note: Grated cheese is not served with this dish.

SPAGHETTI WITH GARLIC AND OLIVE OIL
Spaghetti aglio e olio

(Serves 4)

This is one of the easiest of pasta dishes to prepare and is a must for garlic lovers.

Imperial (Metric)	American
Sea salt	Sea salt
1 lb (450g) wholemeal spaghetti	1 pound wholewheat spaghetti
3 fl oz (90ml) olive oil	⅓ cupful olive oil
2 or more cloves of garlic, peeled and very finely chopped	2 or more cloves of garlic, peeled and very finely chopped
Freshly ground black pepper	Freshly ground black pepper
2 tablespoonsful chopped fresh parsley	2 tablespoonsful chopped fresh parsley

1. Bring a large pan of salted water to a rapid boil. Lower ends of spaghetti into water, pressing them in further around side of pan as ends soften. Boil uncovered for about 12 minutes, or until *al dente* (still firm to the bite).

2. Meanwhile, prepare the sauce, Put the oil and garlic in a small saucepan, cook over a very low heat for 1 or 2 minutes, or until the garlic just begins to colour.

3. Drain the spaghetti, transfer to a warm serving dish and pour in the hot oil and garlic sauce. Toss rapidly, coating all the strands, season with freshly ground black pepper. Garnish with parsley and serve at once.

TAGLIATELLE WITH SWEET PEPPERS
Tagliatelle ai peperoni

(Serves 4)

Imperial (Metric)	American
1 lb (450g) red or yellow peppers, or a mixture of both	1 pound red or yellow peppers, or a mixture of both
2 fl oz (60ml) olive oil	¼ cupful olive oil
1 small onion, finely chopped	1 small onion, finely chopped
14 oz (400g) tin tomatoes, chopped with their juice	1 medium can tomatoes, chopped with their juice
½ teaspoonful raw cane sugar (optional)	½ teaspoonful raw cane sugar (optional)
Sea salt and freshly ground black pepper	Sea salt and freshly ground black pepper
3 fl oz (90ml) dry white wine	⅓ cupful dry white wine
20 black olives, stoned and halved	20 black olives, pitted and halved
2 teaspoonsful fresh basil, chopped (optional)	2 teaspoonsful fresh basil, chopped (optional)
1 lb (450g) wholemeal tagliatelle	1 pound wholewheat tagliatelle

1. Roast the peppers according to the instructions on page 103.

2. Heat the oil in a saucepan and fry the onion until soft. Add the chopped tomatoes with their juice, the sliced peppers, sugar (if used) and salt and pepper to taste.

3. Pour in the wine and bring to the boil. Reduce the heat and simmer, uncovered, for 15-20 minutes, stirring occasionally.

4. Five minutes before the end of the cooking time add the olives. Check the seasoning and stir in the basil, if using.

5. Meanwhile, cook the pasta in boiling salted water until *al dente;* drain well. Turn into a warmed serving dish. Add the sauce, toss and serve immediately.

SPAGHETTI OMELETTE
Frittata di spaghetti

(Serves 4 to 6)

Imperial (Metric)	American
¾ lb (350g) wholemeal spaghetti	12 ounces wholewheat spaghetti
Sea salt	Sea salt
1½ oz (40g) butter or polyunsaturated margarine	3 tablespoonsful butter or polyunsaturated margarine
2 oz (50g) freshly grated Parmesan cheese	½ cupful freshly grated Parmesan cheese
2 tablespoonsful chopped fresh parsley	2 tablespoonsful chopped fresh parsley
3 eggs	3 eggs
Freshly ground black pepper	Freshly ground black pepper
3 fl oz (90ml) olive oil	⅓ cupful olive oil

1. Cook the spaghetti in plenty of boiling salted water until *al dente*. Drain and mix with the butter or margarine, the grated cheese and the parsley. Leave to cool completely, stirring frequently with a fork so it does not stick together.

2. Beat the eggs; season well and pour over the cold spaghetti. Toss thoroughly.

3. Put 4 tablespoonsful of the oil in a large, heavy-based frying pan and when it is hot pour in the spaghetti mixture, spreading it out to an even thickness. Cook over a moderate heat for about 4 or 5 minutes. Try to get the *Frittata* to brown evenly by tilting the pan slightly as it cooks; otherwise it will be overcooked in the middle and undercooked at the edges.

4. When one side of the *Frittata* is crisp and golden slide it onto a plate and return to the pan to cook the other side, adding the remainder of the oil.

5. Place the *Frittata* onto a warm serving dish and serve immediately cut into wedges.

SPAGHETTI WITH COURGETTES
Spaghetti con le zucchine

(Serves 4 to 5)

Imperial (Metric)	American
Sea salt	Sea salt
1 lb (450g) wholemeal spaghetti	1 pound wholewheat spaghetti
3 fl oz (90ml) olive oil	⅓ cupful olive oil
2 cloves of garlic, peeled and sliced	2 cloves of garlic, peeled and sliced
1½ lbs (675g) courgettes	1½ pounds zucchini
Freshly ground black pepper	Freshly ground black pepper
1½ oz (40g) butter, melted	3 tablespoonsful melted butter
6 fresh basil leaves, finely chopped (optional)	6 fresh basil leaves, finely chopped (optional)

1. Bring a large pan of water to a rapid boil (add salt when boiling). Drop in the spaghetti. By the time it is cooked to *al dente,* you will have finished frying the courgettes (zucchini).

2. Meanwhile, cut off and discard both ends of the courgettes (zucchini). Wash, dry well and slice them into thin rounds. Heat the oil in a large, heavy-based frying pan, add the garlic and fry until it is golden; then remove and discard it. Add the slices to the pan and fry with a little salt and freshly ground black pepper until they are tender. Stir frequently so that they do not burn. This should take 8-10 minutes.

3. Drain the spaghetti, place in a warmed serving dish. Pour over the melted butter, the courgettes (zucchini) and their cooking oil and the basil, if using. Toss thoroughly and serve at once.

Note: Grated cheese is not usually served with this dish.

MOULDED PASTA WITH AUBERGINE
Pasta incaciata

(Serves 4)

This dish comes from Sicily where aubergines (eggplants) grow especially well and are used in much of the local cooking.

Imperial (Metric)	American
3 medium aubergines	3 medium eggplants
Sea salt	Sea salt
Wholemeal flour	Wholewheat flour
2 eggs, well beaten	2 eggs, well beaten
1½ oz (40g) freshly grated Parmesan cheese	⅓ cupful freshly grated Parmesan cheese
Olive oil	Olive oil
½ lb (225g) wholemeal 'elbow' macaroni, or similar pasta of your choice	8 ounces wholewheat 'elbow' macaroni, or similar pasta of your choice
3 oz (75g) fresh shelled peas, cooked	½ cupful fresh shelled peas, cooked
2 hard-boiled eggs, chopped	2 hard-boiled eggs, chopped
4 oz (100g) Mozzarella cheese, diced	1 cupful Mozzarella cheese, diced
1½ pints (850ml) Tomato Sauce (pages 129-131)	3¾ cupsful Tomato Sauce (pages 129-131)

1. Wipe the aubergines (eggplants) and trim off the green stalks. Cut lengthwise into ¼ in. (5mm) thick slices, sprinkle with salt and leave in a colander (not metal) for at least 30 minutes so that the bitter juice and excess liquid drains out. Rinse and pat dry.

2. Coat the slices in flour and dip them in the beaten egg mixed with 2 or 3 tablespoonsful of the freshly grated Parmesan cheese. Fry them in very hot oil until crisp and golden on both sides. Drain on absorbent kitchen paper and keep hot.

3. Cook the pasta in plenty of boiling salted water and drain while still quite firm.

4. Grease a deep, round ovenproof dish (e.g. a soufflé dish) with a little oil. Line the bottom and sides with three-quarters of the aubergine (eggplant) slices.

5. In a bowl, mix the cooked pasta with one-third of the Tomato Sauce. Stir in the peas, eggs, Mozzarella and half of the remaining Parmesan cheese. Fill the lined mould with the mixture. Cover with the remaining aubergine (eggplant) slices and spread a little Tomato Sauce over the top.

6. Cover the dish with foil and bake in a fairly hot oven preheated to 375°F/190°C (Gas Mark 5) for 25-30 minutes. Remove the mould from the oven and leave it to settle for 10 minutes. Remove the foil and turn out onto a warm serving dish. Pour over the remaining hot sauce (reheated if necessary) and sprinkle with cheese. Serve immediately.

PASTA SHELLS WITH CAULIFLOWER, GARLIC AND OIL
Conchiglie con salsa di cavolfiore

(Serves 4 to 6)

Imperial (Metric)	American
1 head cauliflower	1 head cauliflower
(about 1 ½ lb/675g)	(about 1 ½ pounds)
Sea salt	Sea salt
3 fl oz (90ml) olive oil	⅓ cupful olive oil
2 cloves of garlic, peeled and crushed	2 cloves of garlic, peeled and crushed
¼ teaspoonful chilli pepper (optional)	¼ teaspoonful chilli pepper (optional)
Freshly ground black pepper	Freshly ground black pepper
1 lb (450g) wholemeal pasta shells	1 pound wholewheat pasta shells
2 tablespoonsful fresh parsley, chopped	2 tablespoonsful fresh parsley, chopped

1. Trim cauliflower and divide into florets. Cook in boiling salted water for about 15-20 minutes or until just tender. Drain and cut into small pieces.

2. Heat the oil in a saucepan, add the onion and garlic and fry until translucent and soft. Stir in the cauliflower, lightly mashing it with a fork to break it up to form a pulp. Add the hot pepper, if using, and salt and pepper to taste, cook for a few minutes more, stirring frequently. Then turn off the heat.

3. Meanwhile, cook the pasta in plenty of boiling salted water until *al dente,* firm to the bite. Drain, and stir the pasta into the pan with the sauce. Toss well. Turn into a warm serving dish. Sprinkle with the chopped parsley and serve immediately.

Note: You can if you wish, reserve the cauliflower water for cooking the pasta.

TAGLIATELLE WITH MUSHROOMS AND CREAM
Tagliatelle con funghi e panna

(Serves 4)

Imperial (Metric)	American
1 lb (450g) button mushrooms	1 pound button mushrooms
2 oz (50g) butter or polyunsaturated margarine	¼ cupful butter or polyunsaturated margarine
2 tablespoonsful olive oil	2 tablespoonsful olive oil
1 clove of garlic, peeled and crushed	1 clove of garlic, peeled and crushed
¼ pint (150ml) double cream	⅔ cupful heavy cream
1 lb (450g) wholemeal tagliatelle	1 pound wholewheat tagliatelle
Sea salt	Sea salt
2 tablespoonsful fresh parsley, chopped	2 tablespoonsful fresh parsley, chopped
Freshly ground black pepper	Freshly ground black pepper

1. Wipe the mushrooms with a damp cloth, or, if they are too dirty, rinse quickly in cold water and dry well. Slice thinly without detaching the stalks. leaving the very small ones whole.

2. Heat the butter and oil in a heavy-based frying pan (skillet) and fry the garlic for a few minutes until soft but not brown. Add the mushrooms and continue to cook over a very low heat, stirring from time to time, for 8-10 minutes. Stir in the cream, season and heat through but do not allow to boil.

3. Meanwhile, cook the tagliatelle in plenty of boiling salted water. When it is *al dente*, drain and return to the pan. Pour over the mushroom and cream sauce, the chopped parsley and a generous quantity of freshly ground black pepper.

4. Toss lightly to coat and turn on to a warmed serving dish. Serve immediately.

PASTA SHELLS WITH PEAS AND RICOTTA
Conchiglie con piselli e ricotta

(Serves 4 to 6)

Imperial (Metric)	American
6 oz (175g) Ricotta cheese	¾ cupful Ricotta cheese
1 oz (25g) freshly grated Parmesan cheese	¼ cupful freshly grated Parmesan cheese
Sea salt	Sea salt
A Pinch of grated nutmeg	A pinch of grated nutmeg
Freshly ground black pepper	Freshly ground black pepper
1 lb (450g) wholemeal pasta shells	1 pound wholewheat pasta shells
6 oz (175g) fresh peas, shelled weight	1 cupful fresh shelled peas
1 oz (25g) butter	2½ tablespoonsful butter

1. Put the Ricotta into the bowl from which the pasta will be served. Beat it with a wooden spoon until smooth, add the grated Parmesan cheese, and season with a little salt, nutmeg and freshly ground black pepper.

2. Meanwhile, cook the pasta in plenty of boiling salted water until *al dente*, (the peas may be cooked with the pasta, but if you are not certain of being able to have them ready at the same moment it is better to cook them in separate pans).

3. Drain the pasta and the peas and mix at once with the Ricotta mixture and the butter. Toss thoroughly, then serve immediately with extra Parmesan cheese passed around separately.

Note: Although pasta shells are recommended, any pasta whose twists or cavities will catch bits of the sauce will do.

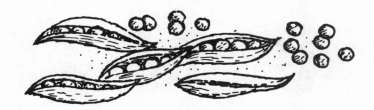

PASTA SPIRALS WITH WALNUT SAUCE
Fusilli in salsa di noci

(Serves 4 to 5)

Imperial (Metric)	American
4 oz (100g) shelled walnuts, chopped	¾ cupful shelled, chopped English walnuts
2 tablespoonsful fresh parsley, finely chopped	2 tablespoonsful fresh parsley, finely chopped
2 tablespoonsful cream or top of the milk	2 tablespoonsful cream or top of the milk
2 tablespoonsful fine wholemeal breadcrumbs	2 tablespoonsful fine wholewheat breadcrumbs
2 tablespoonsful olive oil	2 tablespoonsful olive oil
1 lb (450g) wholemeal pasta spirals	1 pound wholewheat pasta spirals
Sea salt and freshly ground black pepper	Sea salt and freshly ground black pepper
1½ oz (40g) butter or polyunsaturated margarine	3 tablespoonsful butter or polyunsaturated margarine
2 oz (50g) freshly grated Parmesan cheese (optional)	½ cupful freshly grated Parmesan cheese (optional)

1. Spread the walnuts on a baking sheet and place in a preheated oven, 350°F/180°C (Gas Mark 4) for 8-10 minutes. Turn into a clean towel and rub off most of the skin.

2. Grind the walnuts in a blender until they are reduced to a paste. (If you do not have a blender, pound them to a paste using a mortar and pestle.) Put the walnut paste into a bowl and stir in the finely chopped parsley, the cream or milk, the breadcrumbs, and gradually add the oil to produce a sauce the consistency of thick cream. Then season to taste with salt and pepper.

3. Cook the pasta *al dente*, drain it, and mix at once with the butter. Turn into a warmed serving dish. Add the sauce, toss until the pasta is coated, then serve immediately with the Parmesan cheese passed separately, if using.

Note: In Italy the sauce is thinned by adding 3 or 4 tablespoonsful of the cooking water before mixing it with the pasta.

MACARONI WITH MOZZARELLA AND TOMATO SAUCE
Maccheroni alla napoletana

(Serves 4)

Imperial (Metric)	American
3 oz (75g) butter or polyunsaturated margarine	⅓ cupful butter or polyunsaturated margarine
1 medium onion, finely chopped	1 medium onion, finely chopped
1 clove of garlic, peeled and crushed	1 clove of garlic, peeled and crushed
14 oz (400g) tin tomatoes	1 medium can tomatoes
1 teaspoonful raw cane sugar (optional)	1 teaspoonful raw can sugar (optional)
Sea salt and freshly ground black pepper	Sea salt and freshly ground black pepper
¾ lb (350g) wholemeal macaroni	12 ounces wholewheat macaroni
6 oz (175g) Mozzarella or Bel Paese cheese, sliced	1½ cupsful Mozzarella or Bel Paese cheese, sliced

1. Melt two-thirds of the butter or margarine in a saucepan, add the onion and garlic and fry gently until soft. Add the tomatoes with their juice, sugar (if used) and a little salt and pepper and stir with a wooden spoon to break up the tomatoes. Bring to the boil, partially cover and simmer for 25-30 minutes until thick.

2. Cook the macaroni in boiling salted water — undercooking it slightly until barely *al dente*, drain thoroughly.

3. Arrange alternate layers of pasta, sliced Mozzarella or Bel Paese and tomato sauce in an oiled ovenproof dish, ending with a layer of tomato sauce. Dot with the remaining butter or margarine and bake in a preheated moderately hot oven, 400°F/200°C (Gas Mark 6) for about 20-25 minutes.

SPAGHETTI WITH AUBERGINE AND TOMATOES
Spaghetti con melanzane e pomodori

(Serves 4)

Imperial (Metric)	American
1 medium aubergine	1 medium eggplant
Sea salt	Sea salt
1 oz (25g) butter or polyunsaturated margarine	2½ tablespoonsful butter of polyunsaturated margarine
1 lb (450g) ripe tomatoes, blanched, seeded and chopped	1 pound ripe tomatoes, blanched, seeded and chopped
1 clove of garlic, peeled and crushed	1 clove of garlic, peeled and crushed
2 teaspoonsful fresh basil, finely chopped, or 1 teaspoonful dried basil	2 teaspoonsful fresh basil, finely chopped, or 1 teaspoonful dried basil
Freshly ground black pepper	Freshly ground black pepper
Vegetable oil for frying	Vegetable oil for frying
¾ lb (350g) wholemeal spaghetti	12 ounces wholewheat spaghetti

1. Wash and slice the aubergine (eggplant) into rounds about ¼ inch (5mm) thick. Put the slices into a plastic colander and sprinkle a little salt on them, and leave to drain for 30-45 minutes. After that dry them thoroughly with kitchen paper.

2. Meanwhile, melt the butter or margarine in a medium-sized saucepan, add the chopped tomatoes, garlic, basil and seasoning to taste; cook over a low heat for 15 minutes.

3. Heat ½ inch (1 cm) oil in a large, heavy-based frying pan and fry the aubergine (eggplant) slices, a few at a time, until they are crisp and golden brown on both sides. They will absorb the oil quite quickly, so keep adding more oil as needed.

4. Drain on kitchen paper to absorb the excess fat, then cut into halves or quarters and add them to the tomato sauce. Heat through again while the pasta is cooking. Check the seasoning.

5. Cook the spaghetti in plenty of boiling salted water until *al dente*; drain well. Serve the pasta on individual hot plates, with the sauce spooned on top.

HOME-MADE RAVIOLI WITH RICOTTA FILLING
Ravioli con ripieno di ricotta

(Serves 4 to 5 as a main dish)

Imperial (Metric)	American
½ lb (225g) Ricotta or curd cheese	1 cupful Ricotta or curd cheese
1 egg yolk	1 egg yolk
3 tablespoonsful finely chopped, fresh parsley	3 tablespoonsful finely chopped, fresh parsley
2 oz (50g) freshly grated Parmesan cheese	½ cupful freshly grated Parmesan cheese
A pinch of freshly grated nutmeg	A pinch of freshly grated nutmeg
Sea salt and freshly ground black pepper	Sea salt and freshly ground black pepper
1 quantity basic pasta dough (page 38)	1 quantity basic pasta dough (page 38)
¾ pint (425ml) Tomato Sauce (pages 129-131)	2 cupsful Tomato Sauce (pages 129-131)

1. To prepare the filling, mix the Ricotta cheese with the egg yolk, parsley, Parmesan and nutmeg until thoroughly blended. Taste and adjust the seasoning. Put aside until required.

2. Divide the dough into four pieces, and roll each one out to a rectangle of ⅛ inch (3mm) thick. Cover any dough you are not working with a damp cloth to prevent it drying out.

3. Place teaspoonsful of the filling evenly spaced at 1½ inch (4cm) intervals on two sheets of dough. With a pastry brush dipped in cold water dampen the spaces between the mounds of filling to help seal the dough. Uncover the other sheets of pasta and carefully place on top of the fillings.

4. With your index finger, press down along the dampened lines to push out any trapped air and seal well. With either a special ravioli cutter, a serrated-edged pastry wheel or even a sharp knife, cut the ravioli into squares between the pouches. Seal the edges firmly by pressing the seams together all round, either with your fingers or with a fork. Separate the ravioli; place on lightly floured greaseproof paper, and leave to dry for about an hour before cooking. Alternatively, cover with cling film and refrigerate overnight.

5. Cook the ravioli in a large pan of boiling salted water until *al dente* – just firm to the tooth – about 8-10 minutes. Drain and serve immediately with the tomato sauce on top.

Note: You can make ravioli in advance and freeze them. Pack ravioli in a rigid container with greaseproof paper between. Cook from frozen, allowing about 4 minutes extra time.

FETTUCCINE WITH GORGONZOLA SAUCE
Fettuccine al gorgonzola

(Serves 4 to 5)

Imperial (Metric)	American
1½ oz (40g) butter	3 tablespoonsful butter
3 fl oz (90ml) milk	⅓ cupful milk
6 oz (175g) Gorgonzola cheese, broken into small pieces	1½ cupsful Gorgonzola cheese, broken into small pieces
1 lb (450g) home-made fettuccine (page 39)	1 pound home-made fettuccine (page 39)
3 fl oz (90ml) double cream	⅓ cupful heavy cream
Freshly ground black pepper	Freshly ground black pepper
1 oz (25g) freshly grated Parmesan cheese	¼ cupful freshly grated Parmesan cheese

1. Put the butter, milk and Gorgonzola cheese into a large flameproof casserole or an enamelled iron pan, that can later hold all the pasta. Place over a low heat and mash the cheese with a wooden spoon to incorporate the butter and milk to form a creamy sauce. Turn off the heat.

2. Cook the fettuccine in plenty of boiling salted water until *al dente*, firm to the bite. Home-made pasta cooks very quickly – about 3-5 minutes. Drain well.

3. Just before the pasta is cooked, turn on the heat for the sauce. Stir in the cream, season with freshly ground black pepper and heat through but do not allow to boil.

4. Add the drained, cooked pasta to the sauce with the Parmesan cheese and toss lightly to coat. Serve immediately, directly from the pan, with extra Parmesan cheese passed separately.

5. Rice

Rice is grown in vast quantities in the north of Italy, where it is largely cultivated in the Po Valley. Rice is to the northern provinces of Italy (Lombardy, Piedmont and the Veneto) what pasta is to the south, and some northern Italians will have you believe that pasta is not to be found in the north at all. This is not entirely true, but it is a fact that all the best rice dishes come from the north and almost every northern Italian would rather eat rice than spaghetti.

Every rice-growing country has its own special rice dish. In Italy it is the *risotto*. Although the aim in most types of rice cookery is to produce separate grains, without a trace of stickiness, a *risotto* is an exception. *Risotto* is a uniquely Italian technique for cooking rice. It should be moist enough to be poured; its final consistency depends on regular stirring, which agitates the surface starch of the rice so that the grains, still firm to the bite *(al dente)*, are suspended in a creamy liquid. Use brown, round-grain or short grain rice, which is stickier than long-grain rice. Furthermore, its grains withstand the stirring well; long-grain rice is more likely to break. Cooking time varies with the quality of the rice; the better the rice, the longer it takes to cook, as it absorbs more liquid. A *risotto* can be as plain or elaborate as you please, yet they are all produced in the same way. Guidelines are given in the following recipe for making risotto. This is an unorthodox method, but it works well for brown rice.

BASIC RISOTTO
The following outline can be used as a guide for all Risotto recipes

1. Put a large knob of butter or margarine and a little olive oil into a large, heavy-based saucepan. Add a finely chopped onion and cook until it softens, but do not allow it to brown.

2. Rinse the rice carefully, picking out any small stones etc. Add the rice and cook, stirring, for 2-3 minutes to ensure that all the grains are completely coated with the fat and the grains begin to look translucent.

3. Add two-thirds of the hot stock. Cover and cook over a gentle heat for approximately 25 minutes. Then remove the lid and cook uncovered for the rest of the cooking over a fairly lively heat. Continue cooking the rice, stirring all the time and adding more stock as each addition is absorbed. Towards the end of cooking, add the stock in smaller quantities, so that when the rice is cooked to *al dente*, firm to the bite; it will be moist and surrounded by a creamy liquid, not 'swimming' in stock.

4. Remove the pan from the heat and stir in a little more butter or margarine and freshly grated Parmesan cheese. Adjust the seasoning and ladle the *risotto* into shallow soup plates. Serve immediately with extra Parmesan cheese passed separately.

Note: The *risotto's* smoothness is enhanced by the addition of butter and grated Parmesan cheese; the butter and cheese should be added off the heat so the butter does not cook but stays thick and creamy.

RISOTTO WITH COURGETTES
Risotto con le zucchine

(Serves 4)

Imperial (Metric)	American
4 medium courgettes	4 medium zucchini
1 tablespoonful olive oil	1 tablespoonful olive oil
2 oz (50g) butter or polyunsaturated margarine	1/4 cupful butter or polyunsaturated margarine
1 large onion, finely chopped	1 large onion finely chopped
1 clove of garlic, peeled and crushed	1 clove of garlic, peeled and crushed
3/4 lb (350g) short grain brown rice	1 1/2 cupsful short grain brown rice
2 pints (1.15 litres) hot vegetable stock (approx.)	5 cupsful hot vegetable stock (approx.)
Sea salt and freshly ground black pepper	Sea salt and freshly ground black pepper
2 tablespoonsful fresh parsley, chopped	2 tablespoonsful fresh parsley, chopped
1 oz (25g) freshly grated Parmesan cheese	1/4 cupful freshly grated Parmesan cheese

1. Cut off and discard both ends of the courgettes (zucchini) and cut into 1/2 inch (1 cm) thick slices. Set aside.

2. Heat the oil and half the butter or margarine in a heavy-based saucepan, add the onion and fry gently for 3 minutes, then add the garlic and the courgettes (zucchini) and fry until they are a pale golden colour – about 7-10 minutes. Add the rice and cook, stirring, for 2-3 minutes until translucent.

3. Stir in about two-thirds of the hot stock, cover the pan and cook over a very low heat, adding more stock from time to time until the rice is tender but still firm and creamy rather than mushy.

4. Remove the pan from the heat and add the remaining butter or margarine, the chopped parsley, the grated Parmesan, and salt and pepper to taste. Turn onto a warmed serving dish and serve immediately, with a bowl of freshly grated Parmesan cheese passed separately.

RISOTTO WITH MUSHROOMS
Risotto con funghi

(Serves 4)

Imperial (Metric)
1 tablespoonful olive oil
2 oz (50g) butter or
   polyunsaturated margarine
1 large onion, finely chopped
¾ lb (350g) short grain brown rice
¼ pint (150ml) dry white wine
½ lb (225g) mushrooms, sliced
2 tablespoonsful fresh parsley,
   chopped
2 pints (1.15 litres) hot vegetable
   stock (approx.)
Sea salt and freshly ground black
   pepper
1 oz (25g) freshly grated Parmesan
   cheese

American
1 tablespoonful olive oil
¼ cupful butter or
   polyunsaturated margarine
1 large onion, finely chopped
1½ cupsful short grain brown
   rice
⅔ cupful dry white wine
4 cupsful mushrooms, sliced
2 tablespoonsful fresh parsley,
   chopped
5 cupsful hot vegetable stock
   (approx.)
Sea salt and freshly ground black
   pepper
¼ cupful freshly grated
   Parmesan cheese

1. Heat the oil and half the butter or margarine in a heavy-based saucepan, add the onion and fry gently until soft and golden. Add the rice and stir until it is well coated and translucent, about 3 minutes.

2. Pour in the wine and continue to cook, uncovered, over low heat until it has all but evaporated. Stir in the sliced mushrooms and the parsley.

3. Add about two-thirds of the hot vegetable stock, cover the pan and cook over a very low heat, adding more stock from time to time until the rice is tender and the consistency creamy, which will take about 40 minutes.

4. Remove from the heat, stir in the remaining butter or margarine and the cheese. Serve immediately, with extra Parmesan cheese passed separately.

SPINACH RISOTTO
Risotto con spinaci

(Serves 4)

Imperial (Metric)	American
2 oz (50g) butter or polyunsaturated margarine	¼ cupful butter or polyunsaturated margarine
1 large onion, finely chopped	1 large onion, finely chopped
1 lb (450g) fresh spinach, washed and finely chopped	1 pound fresh spinach, washed and finely chopped
¾ lb (350g) short grain brown rice	1½ cupsful short grain brown rice
1½ pints (850ml) hot vegetable stock (approx.)	3¾ cupsful hot vegetable stock (approx.)
2 tablespoonsful olive oil	2 tablespoonsful olive oil
1 clove of garlic, peeled and crushed	1 clove of garlic, peeled and crushed
4 large ripe tomatoes, blanched, seeded and chopped	4 large ripe tomatoes, blanched, seeded and chopped
1 tablespoonful fresh parsley, chopped	1 tablespoonful fresh parsley, chopped
Sea salt and freshly ground black pepper	Sea salt and freshly ground black pepper
Freshly grated Parmesan cheese (optional)	Freshly grated Parmesan cheese (optional)

1. Melt the butter or margarine in a large, heavy-based saucepan, add the onion and fry gently for 5 minutes. Stir in the spinach, cover and cook for 5 minutes more. Add the rice and cook, stirring, for 2-3 minutes until translucent.

2. Stir in about two-thirds of the boiling stock, cover the pan and cook over a very low heat, adding more hot stock from time to time until enough has been absorbed to make the rice tender and moist without being mushy.

3. Towards the end of the cooking time, heat the oil and garlic gently in a saucepan for 2 minutes. Add the tomatoes, parsley, and salt and pepper to taste. Cook briskly for a few minutes until most of the liquid has evaporated and the tomatoes have softened but not reduced to a pulp.

4. Turn the risotto onto a warmed serving dish and pour the sauce into the centre. Serve immediately, with the optional Parmesan cheese passed separately.

COUNTRY-STYLE RISOTTO
Risotto alla paesana

(Serves 4)

Imperial (Metric)	American
3 tablespoonsful olive oil	3 tablespoonsful olive oil
1 onion, finely chopped	1 onion, finely chopped
1 large carrot, finely chopped	1 large carrot, finely chopped
1 celery stick, finely chopped	1 celery stalk, finely chopped
2 medium courgettes, diced	2 medium zucchini, diced
3 oz (75g) fresh peas, shelled weight	½ cupful shelled fresh peas
¾ lb (350g) short grain brown rice	1½ cupsful short grain brown rice
2 pints (1.15 litres) hot vegetable stock (approx.)	5 cupsful hot vegetable stock (approx.)
1 oz (25g) butter or polyunsaturated margarine	2½ tablespoonsful butter or polyunsaturated margarine
Seasoning to taste	Seasoning to taste
2 tablespoonsful fresh parsley, chopped	2 tablespoonsful fresh parsley, chopped
2 oz (50g) freshly grated Parmesan cheese	½ cupful freshly grated Parmesan cheese

1. Heat the oil in a heavy-based saucepan, add all the vegetables and stir constantly until they begin to soften. Add the rice and stir it so that the grains are well coated with the oil.

2. Stir in about two-thirds of the hot stock, cover the pan and cook over a very low heat, adding more hot stock from time to time until the rice is tender but still firm and creamy rather than mushy.

3. After about 40 minutes, when the rice is cooked, remove the pan from the heat. Stir in the butter or margarine, the parsley and the Parmesan cheese. Adjust the seasoning.

4. Turn onto a warmed serving dish and serve immediately, with extra Parmesan cheese passed separately, if desired.

SICILIAN RICE BALLS
Arancini Siciliani

(Makes about 6 to 8 balls)

These crisp-coated and soft-centred rice balls are a very good way of using up leftover cooked rice. To ensure that the rice balls will hold together, make them from rice which has been cooked to a clinging consistency. The remains of a simple risotto are ideal. If possible, make the *arancini* with rice that has been refrigerated – well covered – for at least a day; rice is easiest to mould into rissoles when it is cold.

Imperial (Metric)	American
About 1¼ lb (550g) cooked brown short grain rice	About 3 cupsful cooked brown short grain rice
2 oz (50g) grated Parmesan cheese	½ cupful grated Parmesan cheese
½ pint (275ml) thick Tomato Sauce (pages 129-131)	1⅓ cupsful thick Tomato Sauce (pages 129-131)
2 eggs, well beaten	2 eggs, well beaten
Sea salt and freshly ground black pepper	Sea salt and freshly ground black pepper
2 oz (50g) Mozzarella or Bel Paese cheese	⅓ cupful Mozzarella or Bel Paese cheese
3 oz (75g) fine fresh wholemeal breadcrumbs	1½ cupsful fine fresh wholewheat breadcrumbs
Vegetable oil for deep fat frying	Vegetable oil for deep fat frying
Fresh mint or basil leaves to garnish	Fresh mint of basil leaves to garnish

1. Put the cooked rice into a large bowl. Stir in the Parmesan cheese, 2-3 tablespoonsful of the Tomato Sauce and add enough beaten egg to bind the mixture. (How much beaten egg you use depends on the size of the eggs.) The rice mixture should be quite firm. Add seasoning to taste.

2. Cut the cheese into ½ inch (1 cm) cubes. Take a heaped tablespoonful of the rice mixture and flatten it in the palm of your hand. Put a piece of cheese in the centre, top with another spoonful of rice and form it into a ball about the size of a small orange, so that the cheese is completely enclosed.

3. Roll each ball very carefully, on a plate of fine breadcrumbs. The

balls may be fried at once, but they are easier to handle if refrigerated for at least 30 minutes.

4. Heat the oil in a deep-fat frying pan to 375°F/190°C. If you have no deep frying thermometer, throw in a bread cube; if the bread cube browns in about 1 minute the oil is ready for cooking. Fry the rice balls 3 or 4 at a time until they are crisp and golden – about 4 to 5 minutes – and drain on crumpled kitchen paper. Place in an ovenproof dish in the oven to keep warm while cooking the rest.

5. Just before serving, garnish each 'orange' with a herb leaf. The remaining tomato sauce can be heated through and served separately.

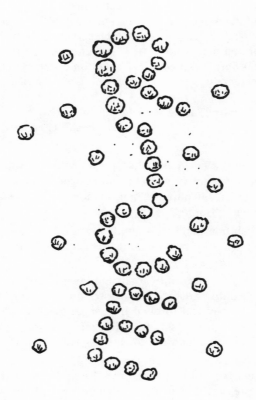

RICE RING WITH MUSHROOMS
Corona di riso con funghi

(Serves 4)

Imperial (Metric)	American
½ lb (225g) short grain brown rice	1 cupful short grain brown rice
Sea salt	Sea salt
1 pint (570ml) water	2½ cupsful water
½ lb (225g) mushrooms	4 cupsful mushrooms
4 tablespoonsful olive oil	4 tablespoonsful olive oil
1 clove of garlic, peeled and crushed	1 clove of garlic, peeled and crushed
2 tablespoonsful fresh parsley, chopped	2 tablespoonsful fresh parsley, chopped
Freshly ground black pepper	Freshly ground black pepper
1½ oz (40g) butter or polyunsaturated margarine	3 tablespoonsful butter or polyunsaturated margarine
1 small onion, finely chopped	1 small onion, finely chopped
½ lb (225g) tin tomatoes	1 small can tomatoes
1 bay leaf	1 bay leaf
1 oz (25g) freshly grated Parmesan cheese	¼ cupful freshly grated Parmesan cheese

1. Put the rice into a heavy-based saucepan with the water. Add ½ teaspoonful of salt and bring to the boil. Cover the pan, reduce the heat and simmer for 40 minutes, or until the rice is tender and all the liquid has been absorbed.

2. Slice the mushrooms and cook gently in the oil for a few minutes. Add the garlic, parsley and seasoning to taste and continue to cook until the mushrooms are soft.

3. Meanwhile, melt half the butter or margarine in a saucepan, add the onion and fry until translucent and soft. Stir in the tomatoes with their juice, the bay leaf (broken into small pieces) and salt and pepper to taste. Cook briskly for a few minutes until most of the liquid has evaporated and the tomatoes have softened.

4. When the rice is cooked stir in the rest of the butter or margarine and the grated Parmesan cheese. Turn the rice into a lightly-oiled ring mould, pressing it down firmly with the back of a spoon. Cover

the mould with foil and bake in a preheated moderate oven, 350°F/180°C (Gas Mark 4) for 10-15 minutes or until heated through. Then unmould on to a warm serving dish and place the mushrooms in the centre and pour the hot sauce all around it. Serve immediately.

CLIVE BIRCH

TIMBALE OF RICE
Timballo di riso

(Serves 4)

Imperial (Metric)	American
2 medium onions	2 medium onions
1 oz (25g) butter or polyunsaturated margarine	2½ tablespoonsful butter or polyunsaturated margarine
¾ lb (350g) short grain brown rice	1½ cupsful short grain brown rice
1½ pints (870ml) hot vegetable stock	3¾ cupsful hot vegetable stock
2 cloves of garlic, peeled and crushed	2 cloves of garlic, peeled and crushed
2 tablespoonsful olive oil	2 tablespoonsful olive oil
1 heaped teaspoonful capers, rinsed	1 heaped teaspoonful capers, rinsed
12 black olives, stoned	12 black olives, stoned
14 oz (400g) tin tomatoes	1 medium can tomatoes
Sea salt and freshly ground black pepper	Sea salt and freshly ground black pepper
1 teaspoonful oregano	1 teaspoonful oregano
4 oz (100g) grated Parmesan cheese	1 cupful grated Parmesan cheese
2 egg yolks	2 egg yolks

1. Peel and chop one of the onions. Melt the butter in a heavy-based flameproof casserole dish, add the onion and fry gently until soft and golden. Add the rice and cook, stirring, for 1 minute until transparent. Pour in the hot stock and bring to the boil. Place in a pre-heated oven at 350°F/180°C (Gas Mark 4) for 45 minutes.

2. Meanwhile, peel and finely chop the remaining onion. Heat the oil in a saucepan, add the onion, garlic and fry for 3 minutes. Add the tomatoes with their juice, the capers, olives, oregano and seasoning to taste. Bring to the boil. Cover and simmer gently for 20 minutes, stirring occasionally.

3. Remove the rice from the oven. Stir in a small knob of butter, the Parmesan cheese and the egg yolks, mix well. Pour the mixture into a lightly oiled deep charlotte mould or soufflé dish. Place in a hot oven at 400°F/200°C (Gas Mark 6) for 10 minutes.

4. Let the timbale of rice settle for 5 minutes, then unmould onto a warmed serving dish and pour on the sauce to serve.

6. Polenta And Gnocchi

Polenta, or maize meal, is one of the staple foods of the north of Italy, particularly of Lombardy and the Veneto regions where it is eaten in all kinds of ways. *Polenta* is economical and nutritious, and provides the basis for a varied number of dishes. Two types of maize meal are used for making it: one is fine and pale, and this is best for dishes where the *polenta* should be quite soft, such as gnocchi. The other is coarse ground and deep yellow, and this produces a much heavier mixture, which is the one most widely used, because of its robust texture. In Italy a special round-bottomed copper pot called a *paiolo* is used for making it but a heavy-based saucepan (preferably copper or cast-iron) is a perfectly good substitute.

I find that plain boiled *polenta* is rather dull and stodgy, but left to get cold and then fried with a little olive oil and a few garlic cloves it is very tasty. It is also particularly good baked in the oven with a little butter and cheese or topped with tomato sauce, or shaped like *gnocchi.*

Gnocchi are small dumplings. They can be made from semolina or mashed potatoes as well as from flour. I have also included recipes for pumpkin *gnocchi* and those made with ricotta and spinach. *Gnocchi* can be made into many small interesting shapes and then poached, fried or baked. They can be eaten as a starter or as part of a main course.

ROMAN GNOCCHI
Gnocchi alla Romana

(Serves 4)

Imperial (Metric)	American
1 pint (570ml) milk	2½ cupsful milk
1 teaspoonful sea salt	1 teaspoonful sea salt
A few twists freshly ground black pepper	A few twists freshly ground black pepper
¼ teaspoonful ground nutmeg	¼ teaspoonful ground nutmeg
6oz (175g) wholemeal semolina	1 cupful wholewheat semolina
3oz (75g) grated Parmesan cheese	¾ cupful grated Parmesan cheese
3oz (75g) butter or polyunsaturated margarine	⅓ cupful butter or polyunsaturated margarine
1 egg, well beaten	1 egg, well beaten

1. Pour the milk into a heavy-based saucepan, season with salt, pepper and nutmeg. Bring to the boil and then slowly pour in the semolina in a steady trickle so that the liquid remains on the boil, otherwise it will form lumps. Lower the heat and begin stirring with a wooden spoon. Continue cooking and stirring until the semolina is so thick that the spoon will stand up unsupported in the middle of the pan. This can take up to 15-20 minutes.

2. Remove the pan from the heat, allow to cool slightly, and stir in two thirds of the Parmesan, one third of the butter or margarine and the beaten egg. When the ingredients are well blended, turn out onto an oiled wooden board or flat dish. Spread with a wet spatula or broad-bladed knife to an overall thickness of about ¼ inch (5mm) and leave until quite cold and firm.

3. Cut the semolina mixture into rounds, squares, lozenges or other shapes using a pastry cutter or knife and arrange these shapes, slightly overlapping each other, in an oiled shallow, ovenproof dish. Dot with flecks of the remaining butter or margarine and sprinkle the remaining cheese on top. Bake in a hot oven preheated to 425°F/220°C (Gas Mark 7) for 15-20 minutes or until a light golden crust has formed. Serve immediately.

RICOTTA GNOCCHI
Gnocchi di ricotta

(Serves 2 to 3)

Imperial (Metric)	American
½ lb (225g) Ricotta or low-fat soft cheese	1 cupful Ricotta or low-fat soft cheese
2 small eggs, beaten	2 small eggs, beaten
1 oz (25g) freshly grated Parmesan cheese	¼ cupful freshly grated Parmesan cheese
4 oz (100g) plain wholemeal flour	1 cupful plain wholewheat flour
A pinch of grated nutmeg	A pinch of grated nutmeg
Sea salt and freshly ground black pepper	Sea salt and freshly ground black pepper
1½ oz (40g) butter	3 tablespoonsful butter

1. Beat the Ricotta or low-fat cheese with a wooden spoon until it is creamy, then add the eggs, Parmesan cheese, flour and a pinch of grated nutmeg. Season with salt and pepper. Mix to a firm paste. Leave for an hour in a cool place, or overnight in the refrigerator, for the mixture to set.

2. Transfer the mixture onto a floured board. Shape into small dumplings, about ½ inch (1 cm) in diameter, in the palm of your hand. Roll them in a little flour.

3. Cook in plenty of boiling unsalted water. Drop them in a few at a time and cook for 3 or 4 minutes. Remove with a slotted spoon as they rise to the surface, then place in a warmed serving dish with melted butter.

4. Serve immediately, sprinkled with extra grated Parmesan cheese.

POTATO GNOCCHI
Gnocchi di patate

(Serves 4 to 6)

Imperial (Metric)	American
2 lbs (900g) floury potatoes[•]	2 pounds floury potatoes[•]
2 eggs, beaten	2 eggs, beaten
¼ teaspoonful grated nutmeg	¼ teaspoonful grated nutmeg
Sea salt and freshly ground black pepper	Sea salt and freshly ground black pepper
½ lb (225g) plain wholemeal flour	2 cupsful plain wholewheat flour

1. Scrub the potatoes. Boil them in their skins until tender. Drain, peel and press through a sieve into a large bowl. Add the eggs, nutmeg and salt and pepper to taste.

2. Gradually add the flour (you may need to use more or less flour depending on the quality of the potatoes, some potatoes absorb more flour than others) then knead thoroughly until very smooth.

3. With floured hands, roll out small portions of the dough into long rolls about the thickness of a finger. Cut into pieces about ¾ inch (2cm) long. Then press them against the curve of a fork to give them the traditional *gnocchi* shape. They cook better if they are slightly concave.

4. Cook the *Gnocchi* a few at a time in plenty of boiling salted water. As soon as they float to the surface they are cooked – this takes 3 or 4 minutes. Remove with a slotted spoon and put into an ovenproof dish and keep hot in a warm oven until they are all cooked.

5. *Gnocchi* may be served with melted butter and a liberal sprinkling of grated Parmesan cheese, or in the Genoese way with Pesto (page 126), or with Tomato Sauce (pages 129-131) – the choice is yours.

[•] Best potatoes to use are Desirée or King Edward potatoes. White potatoes do not make good gnocchi.

PUMPKIN GNOCCHI
Gnocchi di zucca

(Serves 4 to 6)

Imperial (Metric)	American
¾ lb (350g) fresh pumpkin, cubed	12 ounces fresh pumpkin, cubed
Sea salt	Sea salt
2 eggs	2 eggs
1 lb (450g) plain wholemeal flour	4 cupsful plain wholewheat flour
1 oz (25g) butter or polyunsaturated margarine	2½ tablespoonsful butter or polyunsaturated margarine
1½ oz (40g) grated Parmesan cheese	⅓ cupful grated Parmesan cheese

1. Put the cubed pumpkin into a saucepan with 4-5 tablespoonsful of water and season with a pinch of salt. Cover and cook over low heat, stirring occasionally, for about 30 minutes or until the pumpkin cubes have disintegrated. Then push through a sieve over a large bowl. Allow the purée to cool.

2. Add the eggs and mix well. Gradually add the flour to obtain a fairly soft and elastic dough; the amount needed will depend on the ripeness and consistency of the pumpkin. Knead lightly on a floured board.

3. Break off small pieces about the size of a cherry and press them against the curved back of a fork to obtain the traditional *gnocchi* shape.

4. Cook the *gnocchi* in plenty of boiling salted water, uncovered for 5-8 minutes. Remove with a slotted spoon as they rise to the surface. Put in warmed individual bowls and pour over melted butter and sprinkle with Parmesan. Serve immediately.

GNOCCHI WITH CHICK PEAS
Gnocchi con ceci

(Serves 4 to 6)

Imperial (Metric)	American
¾ lb (350g) chick peas, soaked overnight and drained	1½ cupsful garbanzo beans, soaked overnight and drained
Sea salt	Sea salt
1 quantity Potato Gnocchi (page 70)	1 quantity Potato Gnocchi (page 70)
1 pint (570ml) Tomato Sauce made with fresh tomatoes (page 129)	2½ cupsful Tomato Sauce made with fresh tomatoes (page 129)
1 oz (25g) butter or polyunsaturated margarine	2½ tablespoonsful butter or polyunsaturated margarine
Freshly ground black pepper	Freshly ground black pepper
Freshly grated Parmesan cheese (optional)	Freshly grated Parmesan cheese (optional)

1. Put the chick peas (garbanzo beans) in a large heavy-based saucepan and cover them with at least twice their volume of fresh water and bring to the boil. Cook, covered, over a low heat for about 2-3 hours or until the chick peas (garbanzo beans) are soft. Add salt towards the end of the cooking time.

2. Meanwhile, make the potato *gnocchi* and cook in boiling salted water as directed on page 70.

3. When the chick peas (garbanzo beans) are tender, drain off the liquid and put them in a warmed serving dish with the *gnocchi*. Add the butter and pour over the hot Tomato Sauce. Mix well. Season with lots of freshly ground black pepper and serve at once. The cheese, if used, is passed separately.

SPINACH AND RICOTTA GNOCCHI
Gnocchi verdi

(Serves 4 to 6)

Imperial (Metric)	American
3 oz (75g) butter	1/3 cupful butter
1½ lbs (675g) fresh spinach, cooked, squeezed and finely chopped	1½ pounds fresh spinach, cooked, squeezed and finely chopped
½ lb (225g) fresh Ricotta cheese*	½ lb fresh Ricotta cheese*
2 eggs, lightly beaten	2 eggs, lightly beaten
2 oz (50g) plain wholemeal flour	½ cupful plain wholewheat flour
3 oz (75g) grated Parmesan cheese	¾ cupful grated Parmesan cheese
Sea salt and freshly ground black pepper	Sea salt and freshly ground black pepper
A pinch of grated nutmeg	A pinch of grated nutmeg

1. Melt two-thirds of the butter. Add the cooked spinach and cook, stirring continuously, for 3-5 minutes, until almost all the moisture has evaporated and the spinach begins to stick to the pan. Add the Ricotta, or cream and cheese mixture (see note), and cook for a further 2-3 minutes.

2. Transfer the contents of the pan to a large mixing bowl and beat in the eggs, flour and one-third of the Parmesan cheese. Season with salt and pepper and a pinch of nutmeg. Mix well. Cover. Place the mixture in the refrigerator for at least 2 hours or overnight.

3. With lightly floured hands, take about a teaspoonful of the mixture and form into small balls in the palm of your hands.

4. Bring a large pan of salted water to the boil, cook the *gnocchi* a few at a time in the simmering water until they float to the surface (about 2 minutes). Remove with a slotted draining spoon and place in an ovenproof dish. Keep hot in a warm oven until all the *gnocchi* are cooked.

5. Sprinkle with the remaining Parmesan and dot with flecks of butter. Place under a moderate grill, for about 3 minutes, until the cheese has melted. Serve the *gnocchi* immediately.

* Or substitute ½ lb (225g/1 cupful) curd and/or cottage cheese rubbed through a sieve, and 2 tablespoonsful double (heavy) cream.

BASIC METHOD FOR MAKING POLENTA

(Serves 4 to 6)

Imperial (Metric)	American
½ lb (225g) coarse-grained maize meal	2 cupsful coarse-grained corn meal
1 teaspoonful sea salt	1 teaspoonful sea salt
½ pint (275ml) cold water	1⅓ cupsful cold water
1½ pints (850ml) hot water	3¾ cupsful hot water

1. Stir together the maize meal, cold water and salt.

2. Bring the hot water to the boil in a large, heavy-based saucepan. Add the *polenta* mixture, stirring constantly. Reduce the heat and simmer gently for at least 30 minutes, stirring and beating frequently with a stout, long wooded spoon, until the mixture acquires an elastic texture and tears away from the sides of the pan as you stir. A full hour's cooking will produce a softer-textured *polenta*.

3. Turn the *polenta* out immediately it is cooked onto a wet marble slab, an oiled wooden board or flat dish. Flatten it out to an overall thickness of about ½ inch (1cm) using a spatula dipped repeatedly into boiling water to smooth the surface. It can be served at once with butter and cheese, or with Tomato Sauce (pages 129-31), with boiled steamed vegetables; or it can be left until cold, cut into rounds or squares in preparation for subsequent cooking.

Note: If some of the *polenta* should stick to the bottom of the pan, fill with warm water and let it soak for 30 minutes. The *polenta* will then wash away easily.

POLENTA WITH SPRING GREENS AND TOMATO SAUCE
Polenta con verdure e salsa di pomodoro

(Serves 4)

Imperial (Metric)	American
½ lb (225g) maize meal (*polenta*)	2 cupsful corn meal (*polenta*)
Sea salt	Sea salt
¾ pint (425ml) cold water	2 cupsful cold water
1½ pints (850ml) boiling water	3¾ cupsful boiling water
2 tablespoonsful olive oil	2 tablespoonsful olive oil
1 clove of garlic, peeled and crushed	1 clove of garlic, peeled and crushed
14oz (400g) tin tomatoes	1 medium can tomatoes
Freshly ground black pepper	Freshly ground black pepper
¼ teaspoonful raw cane sugar (optional)	¼ teaspoonful raw cane sugar (optional)
1 lb (450g) spring greens	1 pound spring greens
Freshly grated Parmesan cheese (optional)	Freshly grated Parmesan cheese (optional)

1. Prepare the *polenta* as directed in the basic recipe on page 74 with the amount of water listed above to keep it a little thinner.

2. Heat the oil and garlic gently in a saucepan for 2 minutes. Add the tomatoes with their juice, the optional sugar, and salt and pepper to taste. Stir with a wooden spoon to break up the tomatoes. Bring to the boil, partially cover and simmer for 15-20 minutes.

3. Meanwhile, wash and pick over the greens discarding any damaged parts and cut into shreds. Cook in boiling salted water for 5 minutes or until tender. Drain thoroughly and add to the tomato sauce. Stir over a low heat for 5 minutes till the greens are well coated with the sauce. Adjust the seasoning to taste.

4. When the *Polenta* is cooked, pour it onto a large dish. Make a depression in the centre and pour in the greens and all their sauce. Serve immediately with the optional Parmesan cheese passed separately.

BAKED POLENTA WITH ONIONS
Polenta al forno con le cipolle

(Serves 4)

Imperial (Metric)	American
1 quantity *polenta* (page 74)	1 quantity *polenta* (page 74)
3 tablespoonsful olive oil	3 tablespoonsful olive oil
3 medium onions, thinly sliced	3 medium onions, thinly sliced
2 oz (50g) grated Parmesan cheese	½ cupful grated Parmesan cheese
Sea salt and freshly ground black pepper	Sea salt and freshly ground black pepper

1. Prepare the *polenta* as directed in the basic recipe on page 74. Spread out onto a large cold surface to a thickness of about ½ inch (1 cm) and allow it to cool completely and become firm.

2. Heat the oil in a large frying pan, add the onions and fry gently until soft and lightly coloured.

3. Cut the *polenta* into thin slices and place a layer in the base of an oiled ovenproof dish. Cover with a layer of onions, a light sprinkling of cheese and salt and pepper to taste. Repeat the layers until all the *polenta* and onions are used up, finishing with a layer of *polenta* and a final sprinkling of Parmesan. Bake in a preheated moderate oven, 350°F/180°C (Gas Mark 4) for 30 minutes. Serve at once.

POLENTA WITH MUSHROOMS
Polenta con funghi

(Serves 4)

Imperial (Metric)	American
1 quantity *polenta* (page 74)	1 quantity *polenta* (page 74)
2 oz (50g) grated Parmesan cheese	½ cupful grated Parmesan cheese
1 large onion, chopped	1 large onion, chopped
2 tablespoonsful olive oil	2 tablespoonsful olive oil
½ lb (225g) mushrooms, sliced	4 cupsful mushrooms, sliced
¾ pint (425ml) Béchamel Sauce (*Salsa balsamella*) medium-thick (page 124)	2 cupsful Béchamel Sauce (*Salsa balsamella*) medium-thick (page 124)
Sea salt and freshly ground black pepper	Sea salt and freshly ground black pepper

1. Prepare the *polenta* as directed in the basic recipe on page 74 as far as Step 2.

2. Stir half the grated Parmesan cheese into the hot *polenta* Spread out onto a large wet surface to an overall thickness of about ½ inch (1 cm). Allow it to cool completely and become firm.

3. Put the chopped onion with the oil in a frying pan and fry for about 3 minutes, add the mushrooms to the pan and fry for 2 minutes more.

4. In a bowl, mix the contents of the frying pan with the warm sauce. Combine the ingredients well. Check the seasoning.

5. Cut the *polenta* into rounds and place a layer in the base of a well-oiled ovenproof dish and cover with some of the sauce. Repeat the layers, ending with the sauce. Sprinkle with the rest of the grated Parmesan cheese. Bake in a preheated moderately hot oven 375°F/190°C (Gas Mark 5) for 25-30 minutes, or until the cheese and sauce are browned and bubbling. Serve immediately.

POLENTA WITH SAVOY CABBAGE
Polenta con verza

(Serves 4 to 6)

Imperial (Metric)	American
½ Savoy cabbage or other crinkly-leaved winter cabbage, shredded	½ Savoy cabbage or other crinkly-leaved cabbage, shredded
Sea salt	Sea salt
1 quantity *polenta* (page 74)	1 quantity *polenta* (page 74)
4 oz (100g) grated Parmesan cheese	1 cupful grated Parmesan cheese
Plain wholemeal flour for dusting	Plain wholewheat flour for dusting
3 fl oz (90ml) olive oil	⅓ cupful olive oil

1. Cook the cabbage in boiling salted water for 5 minutes. Drain it well. Then stew it in a pan with a little olive oil. Allow to cool.

2. Meanwhile, prepare the *polenta* as directed in the basic recipe on page 74. Stir the cabbage and cheese into the hot *polenta*.

3. Turn it out onto a wooden board or a shallow rectangular dish, and flatten it to a thickness of about 1 inch (2.5cm). Use a spatula that has been coated with olive oil to smooth the surface of the mixture. Leave the mixture to completely cool and become firm for at least 30 minutes.

4. Cut the mixture into large cubes and dust lightly with flour.

5. Heat the remaining oil in a frying pan over a medium heat. When it is hot, put in the cubes, a few at a time, turning them to brown and crisp on both sides. Drain them on absorbent paper and serve at once.

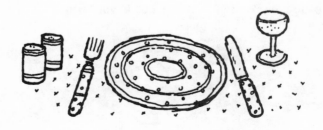

POLENTA GNOCCHI WITH TOMATO SAUCE
Gnocchi di polenta con salsa di pomodoro

(Serves 4)

Imperial (Metric)	American
½ lb (225g) fine maize meal	1½ cupsful fine cornmeal
¼ pint (150ml) cold water	⅔ cupful cold water
1 teaspoonful sea salt	1 teaspoonful sea salt
1 pint (570ml) boiling water	2½ cupsful boiling water
¾ pint (425ml) Tomato Sauce (pages 129-131)	2 cupsful Tomato Sauce (pages 129-131)
1 oz (25g) freshly grated Parmesan cheese	¼ cupful freshly grated Parmesan cheese

1. Combine the maize meal, cold water and salt.

2. Prepare the *polenta* as directed in the basic recipe on page 74. Turn out on a marble slab, an oiled wooded board or large flat dish, and with a spatula dipped in warm water smooth out the *polenta* until it is about ¾ inch (2cm) thick.

3. When it is quite cold and firm cut into round *gnocchi* about 1½ inch (4cm) in diameter with a biscuit cutter (or you can use a small glass). Any trimmings can be kneaded together, rolled and cut into more rounds.

4. Arrange the rounds in an oiled, shallow ovenproof dish, letting them overlap slightly and cover with the tomato sauce. Sprinkle the top with grated Parmesan and bake in a moderately hot oven preheated to 400°F/200°C (Gas Mark 6) for about 20 minutes, until the *polenta* and sauce are heated through and the cheese melts.

7. Pizzas

In Italy I always enjoy watching the *pizzaiolo* (pizza makers) in the Pizzerias. A true *pizzaiolo* never uses a rolling pin, but simply picks up the ball of dough and gradually stretches it, throwing it up in the air and turning it round his fingers! The pizza is then garnished dexterously in a matter of minutes. The pizza is then put on a special wooden peel and pushed into a glowing, wood-fired pizza oven. (Nowadays these are becoming somewhat of a rarity in parts of Italy.) The variety of toppings is almost endless: tomatoes, cheese, onions, garlic, olives, artichokes, mushrooms and peppers are some of the things that are used to give an enormous selection of different pizzas. So when you are your own *pizzaiolo* you can experiment with whatever takes your fancy.

Some cookery books will tell you that pizzas can be made with short crust pastry – of course they can, but they are not at all the same. They can be made quite successfully at home, but they never get that unique taste which the glowing embers of the wood fire give them. In most domestic ovens, the hottest and best place to cook a pizza is right at the top. Discovering the temperature at which your oven best cooks pizzas might be a matter of trial and error; I would suggest you first try it at 450°F/230°C (Gas Mark 8) and never put the pizza in the oven until it has reached its full heat.

Pizza is substantial food, so you may if you wish use 81 or 85 per cent wholemeal flour to produce a lighter base. The dough can also be enriched, if you like, by using milk or half milk and water.

Sometimes the dough is folded over the ingredients to make a turnover or pasty shape called a *calzone*. The word pizza means pie, and I have included in this section a recipe for a double-crusted pizza pie. These are popular throughout Italy and the fillings are numerous. Also included in this section is *focaccia*, a Genoese version of pizza. It is a kind of flatbread, and is particularly good served warm as an appetizer or as table bread. There are many versions of *focaccia*. The simplest is *focaccia all'olio con sale* – a flatbread studded with coarse sea salt. It can be topped with onions or scented with sage or rosemary as described on pages 92-94.

BASIC PIZZA DOUGH

Imperial (Metric)	American
½ oz (15g) fresh yeast or	1 tablespoonful fresh yeast or
¼ oz (7g) dried yeast	½ tablespoonful dried yeast
½ teaspoonful raw cane sugar	½ teaspoonful raw cane sugar
¼ pint (150ml) warm water	⅔ cupful warm water
½ lb (225g) plain wholemeal flour	2 cupsful plain wholewheat flour
1 teaspoonful sea salt	1 teaspoonful sea salt
2 tablespoonsful olive oil	2 tablespoonsful olive oil

1. Dissolve the yeast with the sugar in 3-4 tablespoonsful of the warm water. Leave for 5-10 minutes in a warm place until frothy.

2. Put the flour and salt into a warm bowl, make a well in the centre and pour in the yeast mixture, the rest of the warm water and the olive oil. Mix together until it all comes clean from the sides of the bowl to form a soft but pliable dough, adding a little more water if necessary.

3. Turn out onto a floured surface and knead well for about 5 minutes, until the dough is smooth and fairly elastic.

4. Place in a clean, floured bowl and cover with a damp cloth. Leave in a warm, draughtproof place for about 1½-2 hours until doubled in size.

5. Knock down and knead lightly, then divide the dough into two. Roll out or press each piece into a pizza pan/tray 9 inches in diameter. Pat it gently so that it fits and make the edge of the dough rise a little by tapping it lightly about ½ in. (1 cm) from the edge. (Alternatively place the circles onto oiled baking sheets.)

6. Add topping of your choice. Bake in a preheated oven, 450°F/230°C

(Gas Mark 8). Never put the pizza in the oven until it has reached its full heat.

Note: The quantities suggested will make two 9 inch (23 cm) pizzas or several smaller ones.

PIZZA WITH ONIONS AND OLIVES
Pizza con cipolle e olive

(Serves 2 to 4)

Imperial (Metric)	American
1 quantity risen Pizza dough (page 81)	1 quantity risen Pizza dough (page 81)
2 large onions	2 large onions
3 fl oz (90ml) olive oil	⅓ cupful olive oil
12 black olives	12 black olives
2 tablespoonsful pine nuts	2 tablespoonsful pine kernels
1 teaspoonful dried rosemary	1 teaspoonful dried rosemary
Sea salt and freshly ground black pepper	Sea salt and freshly ground black pepper

1. Shape the dough into individual pizzas as directed on page 81 and set aside.

2. Peel and thinly slice the onions and separate into rings.

3. Brush the dough with half of the oil and cover with the onion rings. Top with the stoned, halved olives, and pine nuts and a sprinkling of rosemary. Season with salt and pepper to taste.

4. Spoon over the remaining oil and bake in a preheated hot oven, 450°F/230°C (Gas Mark 8) for 20 minutes, or until the dough has cooked through. Serve at once.

PIZZA MARGHERITA
Pizza Margherita

(Serves 2 to 4)

Imperial (Metric)	American
1 quantity risen Pizza dough (page 81)	1 quantity risen Pizza dough (page 81)
1 lb (450g) ripe tomatoes, blanched, seeded and chopped	1 pound ripe tomatoes, blanched, seeded and chopped
Sea salt and freshly ground black pepper	Sea salt and freshly ground black pepper
6 oz (175g) Mozzarella cheese, sliced	1 ½ cupful Mozzarella cheese, sliced
4-6 fresh basil leaves, when in season or 1 teaspoonful dried basil	4-6 fresh basil leaves, when in season or 1 teaspoonful dried basil
4 tablespoonsful freshly grated Parmesan cheese	4 tablespoonsful freshly grated Parmesan cheese
1 tablespoonful olive oil (approx.)	1 tablespoonful olive oil (approx.)

1. Prepare the pizza bases as directed on page 81.

2. Spread the tomatoes almost to the edge and season well. Cover with the thinly sliced Mozzarella, then top with the basil and the Parmesan cheese.

3. Sprinkle a little olive oil over the top and place in a preheated hot oven, 450°F/230°C (Gas Mark 8) for 20 minutes, or until the dough has cooked through, and the cheese has melted. Serve immediately.

PIZZA FOUR SEASONS
Pizza quattro stagioni

(Serves 2 to 4)

Imperial (Metric)	American
1 quantity risen Pizza dough (page 81)	1 quantity risen Pizza dough (page 81)
½ lb (225g) tin tomatoes, drained and chopped	1 small can tomatoes, drained and chopped
Sea salt and freshly ground black pepper	Sea salt and freshly ground black pepper
4 oz (100g) mushrooms, sliced	1½ cupsful sliced mushrooms
4 oz (100g) Mozzarella or Bel Paese cheese, sliced	1 cupful Mozzarella or Bel Paese cheese, sliced
½ green pepper, de-seeded and thinly sliced	½ green pepper, de-seeded and thinly sliced
20 black olives, stoned	20 black olives, stoned
2 teaspoonsful oregano	2 teaspoonsful oregano
Olive oil	Olive oil

1. Shape the dough into two discs about 8-9 inches (20-23cm) in diameter. Place the discs on oiled baking sheets.

2. Cover with the tomato almost to the edge and season well. Put the Mozzarella or Bel Paese on one quarter of the pizza, the sliced mushrooms on another, the sliced pepper on a third and the olives on the fourth. Sprinkle with the oregano and a little olive oil.

3. Bake in a preheated hot oven, 450°F/230°F (Gas Mark 8) for 20 minutes. Serve cut into eighths, so that each person has a choice of two flavours, if the pizza is to serve four, or a piece of each, if serving two.

Note: You can divide the pizzas into four sections by reserving a little of the dough, rolling it out into thin strips and placing the strips on the tomato to make a cross.

POLENTA PIZZA
Polenta pizza

(Serves 2 to 4)

This pizza made with a special maize meal base is common in northern Italy. Begin preparing the base in the morning as it needs to stand for several hours to set.

Imperial (Metric)	American
½ lb (225g) fine maize meal	2 cupsful fine corn meal
½ pint (275ml) cold water	1⅓ cupsful cold water
1 teaspoonful sea salt	1 teaspoonful sea salt
1 pint (570ml) boiling water	2½ cupsful boiling water
1 oz (25g) grated Parmesan cheese	¼ cupful grated Parmesan cheese
1 egg	1 egg
2 tablespoonsful olive oil	2 tablespoonsful olive oil
½ lb (225g) tin tomatoes, drained and chopped	1 small can tomatoes, drained and chopped
6 oz (175g) Mozzarella cheese, grated	1½ cupsful Mozzarella cheese, grated
½ lb (225g) mushrooms, sliced	3 cupsful sliced mushrooms
½ teaspoonful oregano	½ teaspoonful oregano
Freshly ground black pepper	Freshly ground black pepper

1. Combine together the maize meal, cold water and salt.

2. Bring water to the boil in a heavy-based saucepan. Add the *polenta* mixture, stirring constantly for about 5 minutes. Reduce the heat and simmer gently for 20 minutes, stirring occasionally, until the *polenta* is thick, smooth and soft. Remove from the heat; add the Parmesan cheese. Allow to cool a little, then beat the egg into the *polenta*.

3. Turn out the mixture into two 8 inch (20cm) lightly-oiled pizza tins. Put aside, uncovered, for several hours until a crust is formed and the surface is fairly dry.

4. Brush the surface of the pizzas with half of the oil, cover with the tomatoes followed by the Mozzarella cheese, and salt and pepper to taste. Top with the mushroom slices and oregano. Sprinkle with the remaining oil and bake in a preheated moderate oven, 350°F/180°C (Gas Mark 4) for 45 minutes. Serve immediately.

SICILIAN PIZZA
Pizza Siciliana

(Serves 4)

Imperial (Metric)	American
1 quantity risen Pizza dough (page 81)	1 quantity risen Pizza dough (page 81)
1 1/4 lbs (550g) ripe tomatoes, blanched, seeded and chopped	1 1/4 pounds ripe tomatoes, blanched, seeded and chopped
Sea salt and freshly ground black pepper	Sea salt and freshly ground black pepper
4 cooked fresh or tinned artichoke hearts	4 cooked fresh or canned artichoke hearts
12 black olives, stoned	12 black olives, stoned
2 cloves of garlic, peeled and sliced	2 cloves of garlic, peeled and sliced
1 teaspoonful oregano	1 teaspoonful oregano
1 tablespoonful olive oil (approx.)	1 tablespoonful olive oil (approx.)
1 oz (25g) freshly grated Parmesan cheese	1/4 cupful freshly grated Parmesan cheese

1. Spread the dough in a 9 × 12 inch (23 × 30cm) baking tray or Swiss-roll tin.

2. Cover with the tomatoes almost to the edge and season well.

3. Slice the artichoke hearts and put on top of the tomato. Add the olives, garlic and oregano.

4. Sprinkle with a little oil and leave to rise in a warm place for 15 minutes.

5. Bake in a preheated hot oven, 425°F/220°C (Gas Mark 7) for about 30 minutes. Because this pizza has a much thicker base and therefore an increased length of cooking time, it is best to add the cheese at *mezzo cottura* – the halfway stage.

Note: This pizza makes a nice change from round ones. It is excellent sliced into small pieces for parties.

PIZZA WITH RICOTTA AND COURGETTES
Pizza con la ricotta e zucchine

(Serves 2 to 4)

Imperial (Metric)	American
1 quantity risen Pizza dough (page 81)	1 quantity risen Pizza dough (page 81)
2 medium courgettes	2 medium zucchini
Sea salt	Sea salt
6 oz (175g) fresh Ricotta or same quantity of curd cheese	¾ cupful fresh Ricotta or same quantity of curd cheese
1 egg	1 egg
1 oz (25g) grated Parmesan cheese	¼ cupful grated Parmesan cheese
2 oz (50g) Fontina cheese, finely grated	½ cupful Fontina cheese, finely grated
Freshly ground black pepper	Freshly ground black pepper
1 tablespoonful fresh parsley, chopped	1 tablespoonful fresh parsley, chopped
Olive oil	Olive oil

1. Shape the dough into circles as directed on page 81 and set aside.

2. Cut off and discard both ends of the courgettes (zucchini). Slice them into very thin discs. Put the slices into a colander, sprinkle a little salt on them, and leave to drain for 25-30 minutes. After that dry them thoroughly with paper towels.

3. In a mixing bowl beat the Ricotta with a wooden spoon. (If using curd cheese, press it through a sieve.) Add the egg, and beat until the mixture is smooth and creamy. Add the grated Parmesan, the chopped parsley, seasoning to taste and mix well.

4. Spread the Ricotta mixture onto the dough; cover with the circles of courgettes (zucchini). Distribute the Fontina evenly over the pizzas. Sprinkle with a little olive oil and bake in a hot oven, 450°F/230°C (Gas Mark 8) for 25 minutes, or until dough is cooked. Serve hot or at room temperature.

BATAVIA AND BLACK OLIVE PIE
Tortino ripieno di scarole e olive

(Makes one 9-10 inch/23-25cm pie)

This is a traditional pizza that is eaten on Christmas Eve in many parts of Italy.

For the dough:

Imperial (Metric)	American
½ oz (15g) fresh yeast or ¼ oz (7g) dried yeast	1 tablespoon fresh yeast or ½ tablespoonful dried yeast
1 teaspoonful raw cane sugar	1 teaspoonful raw cane sugar
⅓ pint (200ml) warm water	¾ cupful warm water
¾ lb (350g) strong plain wholemeal flour	3 cupsful strong plain wholewheat flour
1 teaspoonful sea salt	1 teaspoonful sea salt
3 tablespoonsful olive oil	3 tablespoonsful olive oil
1 egg, well beaten	1 egg, well beaten

For the filling:

Imperial (Metric)	American
1 large head Batavian endive, washed and shredded	1 large head Batavian chicory, washed and shredded
3 fl oz (90ml) olive oil	⅓ cupful olive oil
1 oz (25g) pine nuts	¼ cupful pine kernels
2 oz (50g) sultanas, rinsed and drained	⅓ cupful golden seedless raisins, rinsed and drained
1 tablespoonful capers, rinsed	1 tablespoonful capers, rinsed
4 oz (100g) black olives, stoned and chopped	1 cupful black olives, stoned and chopped
1 clove of garlic, peeled and crushed	1 clove of garlic, peeled and crushed
2 tablespoonsful fresh parsley, chopped	2 tablespoonsful fresh parsley, chopped
Sea salt and freshly ground black pepper	Sea salt and freshly ground black pepper

1. Proceed as for the basic Pizza dough on page 81 with the above ingredients.
2. Heat 4 tablespoonsful of the olive oil in a heavy-based saucepan

over a moderate heat; add the shredded Batavian endive (chicory), reduce the heat and cook for 3-4 minutes, stirring occasionally, until most of the liquid in the pan has evaporated. Add the pine nuts, sultanas (golden seedless raisins), capers, black olives, garlic, parsley and seasoning to taste. Take the pan off the heat and allow to cool completely; this will improve the flavour.

3. When dough has risen, punch down and knead lightly. Roll out two-thirds of the dough and use to line a lightly oiled 9-10 inch (23-25 cm) springform or loose-bottom cake tin: its edges should come half way up the sides of the tin. Spread the filling evenly over the dough. With the tip of a knife, turn the edge of the dough inwards, over the filling, to form a rim. Brush the rim with water to make it sticky.

4. Cover with the remaining piece of dough, rolled out to fit over the top. With your fingers crimp the edges of the dough together to seal in the filling. Prick the top dough with a fork, making holes about 1 inch (2.5 cm) apart all over the top (necessary as air vents). Be careful not to pierce the bottom dough. Brush the top with the remaining oil, cover with a tea towel and allow to rest in a warm place for 15 minutes.

5. Brush the top of the pie with beaten egg to glaze. Bake in a preheated oven 375°F/190°C (Gas Mark 5) for 45-60 minutes, or until golden-brown and well risen. Serve warm, cut into wedges.

BROCCOLI CALZONE
Calzone di broccoli

(Serves 6)

For the dough:

Imperial (Metric)	American
½ oz (15g) fresh yeast or	1 tablespoonful fresh yeast or
¼ oz (7g) dried yeast	½ tablespoonful dried yeast
1 teaspoonful raw cane sugar	1 teaspoonful raw cane sugar
⅓ pint (200ml) warm water	¾ cupful warm water
¾ lb (350g) plain wholemeal flour	3 cupsful plain wholewheat flour
1 teaspoonful sea salt	1 teaspoonful sea salt
2 tablespoonsful olive oil	2 tablespoonsful olive oil

For the filling:

Imperial (Metric)	American
½ lb (225g) broccoli heads	8 ounces broccoli heads
Sea salt	Sea salt
3 tablespoonsful olive oil	3 tablespoonsful olive oil
1 small onion, finely chopped	1 small onion, finely chopped
1 clove of garlic, peeled and crushed	1 clove of garlic, peeled and crushed
6 oz (175g) Provolone or Cheddar cheese, diced	1½ cupsful Provolone or Cheddar cheese, diced
Freshly ground black pepper	Freshly ground black pepper

1. Proceed as for Pizza dough on page 81 with the above ingredients. About 30 minutes before the dough is fully risen, prepare the filling.

2. Trim broccoli leaves and coarse stems, then cook in boiling salted water for about 8-10 minutes. Drain well, then chop and place in a bowl.

3. Gently fry the onion and garlic in a little of the oil until translucent and soft. Add to the bowl with the broccoli, Provolone cheese and the remainder of the olive oil. Season with salt and pepper to taste. Stir until the ingredients are thoroughly blended.

4. On a floured surface knock down the risen dough. Divide it into 6 equal portions and roll out in rounds about ¼ inch (5mm) thick. Leaving a ¼ inch (5mm) margin at the outer edge, spread the filling over half the dough. Moisten the edges with water. Fold the plain

half over the filling to make a pasty or turnover shape. To seal the
filling, crimp the circular edges of the dough firmly together. Place
on a large, oiled baking sheet.

5. Prick the top dough with a fork here and there all over (necessary for
   air vents). Be careful not to pierce the bottom dough. If you like,
   lightly brush the surface of the dough with olive oil. Bake in a
   preheated hot oven 425°F/220°C (Gas Mark 7) for 25 minutes or
   until crisp and golden brown. Serve hot or cold.

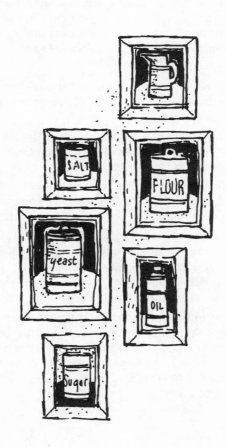

ONION FLATBREAD
Focaccia con le cipolle

(To make one 12 × 9 inch/30 × 23 cm flatbread)

Imperial (Metric)	American
½ oz (15g) fresh yeast or	1 tablespoonful fresh yeast or
¼ oz (7g) dried yeast	½ tablespoonful dried yeast
1 teaspoonful raw cane sugar	1 teaspoonful raw cane sugar
⅓ pint (200 ml) warm water	¾ cupful warm water (approx.)
(approx.)	3 cupsful plain wholewheat flour
¾ lb (350g) plain wholemeal flour	1 teaspoonful fine sea salt
1 teaspoonful fine sea salt	⅓ cupful olive oil
3 fl oz (90 ml) olive oil	1 medium onion, thinly sliced
1 medium onion, thinly sliced	Coarse sea salt
Coarse sea salt	

1. Dissolve the yeast with the sugar in 3-4 tablespoonsful of warm water. Leave for about 10 minutes in a warm place until frothy.

2. Place the flour in a warm bowl with the fine sea salt. Make a well in the centre and pour in the yeast mixture, half the oil and the remaining water. Mix together until it comes clean away from the sides of the bowl to form a firm dough.

3. Turn out onto a floured surface and knead well for about 5 minutes until the dough is smooth. Place in a bowl, cover with a damp cloth or clingfilm, until double in size (about 1½ hours).

4. When the dough has risen, knock down and lightly knead for a few minutes. Roll out the dough into a rectangle about 12 × 9 inch (30 × 23 cm) and place it on an oiled baking sheet or Swiss-roll tin. It should be around ½ inch (1 cm) thick. Leave it to rise a second time for 45 minutes or until light and spongy.

5. Roughen the surface of the dough by dimpling it here and there with your fingertips. Spread the onions over it, pressing them lightly into the dough. Spoon the remaining olive oil over the onions. Sprinkle with a generous pinch of coarse sea salt and bake in a preheated hot oven, 400°F/200°C (Gas Mark 6) for 25-30 minutes or until golden. Serve while still warm.

SAGE FLATBREAD
Focaccia alla salvia

(Makes one 10 inch/25cm round *focaccia*)

Imperial (Metric)	American
½ oz (15g) fresh yeast or ¼ oz (7g) dried yeast	1 tablespoonful fresh yeast or ½ tablespoonful dried yeast
1 teaspoonful raw cane sugar	1 teaspoonful raw cane sugar
⅓ pint (200ml) warm water (approx.)	¾ cupful warm water (approx.)
¾ lb (350g) plain wholemeal flour	3 cupsful plain wholewheat flour
1 teaspoonful fine sea salt	1 teaspoonful fine sea salt
4 tablespoonsful olive oil	4 tablespoonsful olive oil
10 fresh sage leaves, finely chopped, or 2 teaspoonsful dried sage leaves, crumbled	10 fresh sage leaves, finely chopped, or 1 tablespoonful dried sage leaves, crumbled

1. Make the dough according to the instructions for Onion Flatbread on page 92 with the above ingredients.

2. When it has doubled in size, knock the dough down and knead again adding the sage. Make sure the sage is evenly distributed, not all bunched up in one spot. Roll out the dough into a round about 10 inches (25cm) in diameter and place on an oiled baking sheet. It should be about ½ inch (1 cm) thick. If you like your *focaccia* thicker and chewier, roll it out into a slightly smaller circle. Leave it to rise once more in a warm place for about 45 minutes, or until light and spongy.

3. Dimple the surface of the dough here and there with your fingertips and sprinkle the dough with the remaining olive oil.

4. Bake the *focaccia* in an oven preheated to 400°F/200°C (Gas Mark 6) for about 25-30 minutes or until the surface is golden. Serve lukewarm or at room temperature.

ROSEMARY FLATBREAD
Focaccia al rosmarino

This is another lovely flavoured herb bread that is delicious both as a snack and as tasty table bread. To make it, follow the instructions for *focaccia* with sage (see preceding recipe), except that for the sage you will need to substitute about 2 teaspoonsful dried rosemary leaves or 1½ teaspoonsful fresh rosemary, chopped.

8. Vegetables
Le Verdure

The Italians grow an enormous variety of vegetables, so it is hardly surprising that they feature strongly in Italian cooking. Vegetables are always fresh, young and imaginatively cooked. Many vegetables are served as separate dishes in their own right, sometimes before, and sometimes after, the main course. Vegetables are rarely simply boiled, instead they are flavoured with fresh herbs, sauces and other seasonings. Very often spinach, beet and chard (turnip tops), broccoli and similar vegetables are served cold or lukewarm as side dishes, dressed with olive oil and a little lemon juice or vinegar, and very good they are too.

VEGETABLE LOAF
Sformato di verdure

(Serves 4)

Imperial (Metric)	American
1 lb (450g) potatoes	1 pound potatoes
Sea salt	Sea salt
1½ oz (40g) butter or polyunsaturated margarine	3 tablespoonsful butter or polyunsaturated margarine
½ lb (225g) French beans	8 ounces string beans
2 tablespoonsful olive oil	2 tablespoonsful olive oil
1 clove of garlic, peeled and crushed	1 clove of garlic, peeled and crushed
½ lb (225g) carrots, finely grated	1 cupful finely grated carrots
1 celery stick, chopped	1 celery stalk, chopped
1 large onion, finely grated	1 large onion, finely grated
4 oz (100g) mushrooms, sliced	2 cupsful mushrooms, sliced
2 tablespoonsful chopped fresh parsley	2 tablespoonsful chopped fresh parsley
2 oz (50g) grated Parmesan cheese	½ cupful grated Parmesan cheese
2 eggs, lightly beaten	2 eggs, lightly beaten
Freshly ground black pepper	Freshly ground black pepper

1. Scrub the potatoes and boil them in their skins in salted water. When tender, peel and mash while still hot, adding ⅔ of the butter or margarine.

2. Meanwhile, top and tail beans, remove strings if necessary. Cook in boiling salted water for 15 minutes. Drain and chop into small pieces about ½ inch (1cm) in length.

3. Heat the oil in a saucepan, add the garlic, carrots, celery and onion and fry gently for 10 minutes, stirring occasionally. Then add the mushrooms and parsley and cook for a further 5 minutes. Remove from the heat and stir in cooked beans.

4. In a large bowl, mix together the fried vegetables, potatoes, cheese and beaten eggs. Add salt and pepper to taste. Mix well. Pour the mixture into an oiled loaf tin. Dot with small flecks of butter and bake in an oven preheated to 350°F/180°C (Gas Mark 4) for about 35-40 minutes.

5. Remove from oven, leave to stand for 5 minutes, then invert on to a warmed serving plate. Serve hot.

BAKED STUFFED PEPPERS
Peperoni imbottiti

(Serves 4)

Imperial (Metric)	American
4 medium red or green peppers	4 medium red or green peppers
2 tablespoonsful olive oil	2 tablespoonsful olive oil
1 medium onion, finely chopped	1 medium onion, finely chopped
1 clove of garlic, peeled and crushed	1 clove of garlic, peeled and crushed
2 small courgettes, coarsely grated	2 small zucchini, coarsely grated
4 oz (100g) mushrooms, sliced	1½ cupsful sliced mushrooms
2 tablespoonsful chopped fresh parsley	2 tablespoonsful chopped fresh parsley
4 oz (100g) fresh wholemeal breadcrumbs	2 cupsful fresh wholewheat breadcrumbs
2 oz (50g) grated Parmesan cheese	½ cupful grated Parmesan cheese
1 egg, beaten	1 egg, beaten
Sea salt and freshly ground black pepper	Sea salt and freshly ground black pepper

1. Cut a slice off the tops of the peppers. Remove the white pith and the seeds. Parboil the peppers for 3 minutes in boiling water; remove and drain.

2. Heat the oil in a frying pan, add the onion, garlic and grated courgettes (zucchini) and fry for 5 minutes. Add the mushrooms, then stir in the parsley, breadcrumbs, cheese, egg, and salt and pepper to taste. Combine the ingredients thoroughly.

3. Fill the peppers with the mixture, replace the tops and stand them upright (cutting a small slice off the bottom if necessary) in an ovenproof dish with 2 or 3 tablespoonsful of water in the bottom.

4. Bake in a moderate oven 350°F/180°C (Gas Mark 4) for 30-45 minutes, or until the peppers are tender. Serve hot.

POTATO CROQUETTES
Crocchette di patate

(Makes about 16 croquettes)

Imperial (Metric)	American
1½ lbs (675g) potatoes	1½ pounds potatoes
Sea salt	Sea salt
1 egg yolk	1 egg yolk
½ oz (15g) grated Parmesan cheese	2 tablespoonsful grated Parmesan cheese
1 tablespoonful fresh parsley, chopped	1 tablespoonful fresh parsley, chopped
Pinch of grated nutmeg	Pinch of grated nutmeg
1 oz (25g) wholemeal flour	¼ cupful wholewheat flour
1 egg, beaten	1 egg, beaten
2 oz (50g) fresh wholemeal breadcrumbs	1 cupful fresh wholewheat breadcrumbs
Vegetable oil for frying	Vegetable oil for frying

1. Scrub the potatoes; do not peel. Boil them in slightly salted water until tender. Drain. Peel while still hot and mash through a fine sieve into a bowl.

2. Mix the egg yolk into the potatoes. Add the cheese, parsley, salt and nutmeg.

3. When the mixture is cool, divide it into about 14-16 equal portions. Roll each portion on a floured board, gently shaping it by hand into a cylinder. Dip each croquette in beaten egg, then roll it in breadcrumbs.

4. Heat the oil in a deep pan to 350°F(180°C) – test the temperature either with a thermometer or drop in a small cube of bread and if it turns golden and crisp in one minute it is hot enough. Fry the croquettes for 4-5 minutes until golden brown. You will probably need to do the frying in 2 or 3 separate batches. When cooked, drain on absorbent kitchen paper.

BROCCOLI WITH GARLIC
Broccoli all'aglio

(Serves 4-6 as a side dish)

Imperial (Metric)	American
1½ lbs (675g) fresh broccoli heads	1½ pounds fresh broccoli heads
Sea salt	Sea salt
2 cloves of garlic, crushed	2 cloves of garlic, crushed
4 tablespoonsful olive oil	4 tablespoonsful olive oil
2 tablespoonsful fresh parsley, chopped	2 tablespoonsful fresh parsley, chopped
Freshly ground black pepper	Freshly ground black pepper

1. Wash and trim the broccoli heads. Divide into small spears. Cook gently in slightly salted boiling water for 7-10 minutes. The spears must be slightly undercooked (test with a fork). Drain well.

2. Heat the oil in a large frying pan and add the garlic. As soon as the garlic browns slightly, add the broccoli, the chopped parsley and seasoning to taste. Turn the broccoli two or three times while cooking. Serve immediately.

CARROT PURÉE
Pure di carote

(Serves 4 as a side dish)

Imperial (Metric)	American
2 lbs (900g) carrots	2 pounds carrots
1 large potato, peeled and diced	1 large potato, peeled and diced
2 oz (50g) butter	¼ cupful butter
½ oz (15g) grated Parmesan cheese (optional)	2 tablespoonsful Parmesan cheese (optional)
1 tablespoonful chopped fresh parsley	1 tablespoonful chopped fresh parsley
Sea salt	Sea salt

1. Wash and scrub the carrots. Cut them in half lengthwise. Cook in slightly salted water for about 30 minutes or until tender. After 15 minutes add the diced potato.

2. When the vegetables are cooked, drain thoroughly. Purée the carrots through a mouli-legumes or, alternatively, place the vegetables in a food processor with some of the cooking liquid. To the purée add the butter and the cheese, if used. Season to taste.

3. Pour the mixture into an ovenproof dish. Then place in a preheated oven 350°F/180°C (Gas Mark 4) for 10 minutes. Just before serving garnish with chopped parsley.

BRAISED FENNEL TUSCAN STYLE
Finocchio alla Toscano

(Serves 4)

Imperial (Metric)	American
4 fennel bulbs (about 1½ lb/675g)	4 fennel bulbs (about 1½ pounds)
4 tablespoonsful olive oil	
1 large or 2 small cloves of garlic, peeled and sliced	4 tablespoonsful olive oil
Sea salt and freshly ground black pepper	1 large or 2 small cloves of garlic, peeled and sliced
¾ pint (425ml) vegetable stock or water (approx.)	Sea salt and freshly ground black pepper
	2 cupsful vegetable stock or water (approx.)

1. Cut off the tops of the fennel, reserving their feathery leaves to sprinkle over the dish just before serving. Trim away any bruised, discoloured parts from the bulbs. Rinse under running cold water and dry. Halve each bulb lengthwise, or cut into quarters if they are large or if you wish to reduce the cooking time.

2. Place the fennel pieces, flat-side down, in a wide, heavy-based pan together with the oil, garlic and a light sprinkling of salt and freshly ground black pepper. Cook over a moderate heat for at least 10 minutes, turning them over from time to time, until the fennel pieces are well browned.

3. Pour in enough of the stock or water to barely cover the fennel pieces and bring to the boil. Cover and simmer over a very low heat for a further 30-45 minutes or until fennel is tender and the liquid absorbed.

4. If liked, sprinkle fennel with grated Parmesan cheese. Garnish with fennel leaves and serve immediately.

CAULIFLOWER OMELETTE
Frittata di cavolfiore

(Serves 4)

Imperial (Metric)	American
6 large eggs	6 large eggs
¾ lb (350g) cauliflower, cooked until just tender, finely chopped	2 cupsful cauliflower, cooked until just tender, finely chopped
Sea salt and freshly ground black pepper	Sea salt and freshly ground black pepper
2 oz (50g) grated Parmesan cheese	½ cupful grated Parmesan cheese
1½ oz (40g) butter or polyunsaturated margarine	3 tablespoonsful butter or polyunsaturated margarine
1 tablespoonful olive oil	1 tablespoonful olive oil

1. Lightly beat the eggs in a medium-sized bowl, just enough to mix the whites and the yolks. Add the finely chopped cauliflower, salt, pepper and grated Parmesan cheese, and mix thoroughly.

2. Heat the butter and oil in a large, heavy-based frying pan. Pour the egg-and-cauliflower mixture into the pan and cook the *frittata* slowly over a very low heat.

3. When the eggs have set and thickened and only the top is runny put the frying pan under a preheated grill for 30 seconds or until the top of the omelette is cooked, but not browned.

4. Loosen the *frittata* with a spatula and slide it onto a warm serving plate. Cut into wedges and serve immediately.

ROASTED PEPPERS
Peperoni arrostiti

(Serves 4 to 6)

Imperial (Metric)	American
4 large red peppers	4 large red peppers
2 cloves of garlic, peeled and sliced	2 cloves of garlic, peeled and sliced
4 tablespoonsful olive oil	4 tablespoonsful olive oil
Sea salt and freshly ground black pepper	Sea salt and freshly ground black pepper

1. Wash and dry peppers. Place them whole under a moderately hot grill or resting over the flames of a gas burner, turning them frequently until all the skin is charred and blistered. (In Italy they are put directly onto a glowing charcoal fire). This process will take from 15 to 20 minutes depending on the size of the peppers and the heat of the grill. Place peppers in a paper bag. Close tightly. Set aside for 10 minutes. This process makes removing their skins easier. Rub off the blackened skins.

2. Cut each pepper in half lengthwise, remove stalks and seeds and then cut them into ½ inch (1 cm) wide strips.

3. Place peppers in a medium-sized bowl. Add the garlic, olive oil, and salt and pepper to taste. Toss and set aside for at least 30 minutes before serving. Roasted peppers are delicious eaten with wholemeal bread as a sandwich.

COUNTRY MUSHROOM BAKE
Funghi alla paesana

(Serves 4)

Imperial (Metric)	American
1 lb (450g) fresh mushrooms, sliced	6 cupsful sliced fresh mushrooms
Juice of half a lemon	Juice of half a lemon
2 lbs (900g) potatoes	2 pounds potatoes
4 cloves of garlic	4 cloves of garlic
Olive oil	Olive oil
1 oz (25g) fresh parsley	½ cupful fresh parsley
Sea salt and freshly ground black pepper	Sea salt and freshly ground black pepper
1 pint (570ml) milk	2½ cupsful milk
1 oz (25g) butter	2½ tablespoonsful butter
2 tablespoonsful grated Parmesan cheese (optional)	2 tablespoonsful grated Parmesan cheese (optional)

1. In a bowl, place mushroom slices, lemon juice, and enough water to cover. Set aside for 10 minutes to marinate, then drain thoroughly.

2. Peel the potatoes and slice thinly (use a wooden mandolin for best results). Rinse them in cold water to get rid of some of the starch. Dry them on absorbent kitchen paper.

3. Finely chop the parsley and garlic together.

4. Arrange half of the potatoes in the bottom of a buttered ovenproof dish neatly in layers, followed by a sprinkling of oil and a seasoning of salt and freshly ground black pepper. Then add the mushroom slices, garlic and parsley. Finish off with the remaining potato slices.

5. Pour in the milk, and fleck the surface all over with dots of butter. Cook in a moderate oven at 350°F/180°C (Gas Mark 4) for 45 minutes or until the potatoes are cooked and the top layer is nicely golden-brown. If liked, Parmesan cheese may be sprinkled over the potatoes before baking.

BAKED AUBERGINES WITH PARMESAN
Melanzane alla parmigiana

(Serves 4)

Imperial (Metric)	American
4 medium aubergines (approx. 1½ lbs/675g)	4 medium eggplants (approx. 1½ pounds)
Sea salt	Sea salt
Plain wholemeal flour	Plain wholewheat flour
3 fl oz (90ml) olive oil (approx.)	⅓ cupful olive oil (approx.)
¾ pint (425ml) Tomato Sauce (pages 129/131)	2 cupsful Tomato Sauce (pages 129/131)
½ lb (225g) Mozzarella or Bel Paese cheese, thinly sliced	8 ounces Mozzarella or Bel Paese cheese, thinly sliced
2 oz (50g) grated Parmesan cheese	½ cupful grated Parmesan cheese
Freshly ground black pepper	Freshly ground black pepper

1. Remove stalks from aubergines (eggplants) and cut lengthwise into ¼ inch (5mm) thick slices, Place them in a colander, sprinkle generously with salt (this removes their bitterness and draws out moisture) leave to drain for 1 hour, then rinse and pat dry. Dip each slice in flour and shake off the excess.

2. Heat half the oil in a large, heavy-based frying pan and fry the aubergine (eggplant) slices briskly (to prevent them from soaking up too much oil) until golden on both sides. Drain on kitchen paper and keep warm.

3. Cover the bottom of an oiled ovenproof dish with a little sauce. Place a layer of aubergine (eggplant) slices on top followed with a layer of Mozzarella or Bel Paese cheese, a sprinkling of Parmesan and freshly ground black pepper. Repeat these layers until all the ingredients have been used up, ending with Parmesan.

4. Sprinkle a little oil over the top and bake in a moderately hot oven preheated to 400°F/200°C (Gas Mark 6) for 15-20 minutes, until crisp and golden.

SPINACH PUDDING
Sformato di spinachi

(Serves 4)

Imperial (Metric)	American
1½ lbs (675g) fresh spinach	1½ pounds fresh spinach
2 oz (50g) butter or polyunsaturated margarine	¼ cupful butter or polyunsaturated margarine
1 small onion, finely chopped	1 small onion, finely chopped
1 oz (25g) plain wholemeal flour	¼ cupful plain wholewheat flour
⅓ pint (200ml) milk	¾ cupful milk
1 oz (25g) grated Parmesan cheese	¼ cupful grated Parmesan cheese
3 eggs, separated	3 eggs, separated
Sea salt and freshly ground black pepper	Sea salt and freshly ground black pepper
Freshly grated nutmeg	Freshly grated nutmeg
½ pint (275ml) *Salsa di pomodoro* (pages 129-131)	1⅓ cupsful *Salsa di pomodoro* (pages 129-131)

1. Wash the spinach, discard any coarse stalks or discoloured leaves and put into a saucepan with only the water that clings to it. Cover and cook for 7 minutes. Drain and squeeze out all the liquid.

2. Melt half the butter or margarine in a saucepan, add the onion and fry gently for 5 minutes. Add the spinach and cook uncovered, for 2-3 minutes, until the moisture has evaporated.

3. In a separate saucepan, melt the remaining butter or margarine, add the flour and cook for 1 minute. Remove from the heat and gradually stir in the milk. Return to the heat and cook, stirring for 2 minutes, until thick and smooth.

4. Remove the pan from the heat and beat in the spinach, cheese, egg yolks and salt, pepper and nutmeg to taste. Whisk the egg whites until they form soft peaks and fold carefully into the mixture.

5. Pour the mixture into a well-oiled 2½ pint (1.5 litre) pudding basin or mould and cover with a sheet of greaseproof paper.

6. Place in a roasting pan and pour enough hot water to come two-thirds of the way up the mould. Cook in a preheated moderate oven, 350°F/180°C (Gas Mark 4). The *sformato* is cooked when it is firm to

the touch; allow about 1 hour. Let the pudding settle for 5 minutes, then peel off the greaseproof paper and invert onto a warmed serving dish. Spoon the hot Tomato Sauce over and serve immediately.

CLIVE BIRCH

SICILIAN BROAD BEANS
Fave alla Siciliana

(Serves 4)

This dish of braised artichokes, broad beans and peas, is a particular speciality of Palermo.

Imperial (Metric)	American
3-4 medium globe artichokes	3-4 medium globe artichokes
½ lemon	½ lemon
4 tablespoonsful olive oil	4 tablespoonsful olive oil
1 onion, chopped	1 onion, chopped
1 tablespoonful fennel leaves, chopped	1 tablespoonful fennel leaves, chopped
Sea salt and freshly ground black pepper	Sea salt and freshly ground black pepper
2 lbs (900g) fresh broad beans (unshelled weight)	2 pounds fresh Windsor beans (unshelled weight)
1 lb (450g) fresh peas (unshelled weight)	1 pound fresh peas (unshelled weight)

1. Wash the artichokes in salted water. Cut off the stalks at the base of the leaves and trim off the tops of the leaves so that the artichokes are about 2 inches (5cm) high. Then slice the artichokes lengthwise into ½ inch (1cm) wedges. Remove the choke and rub the cut surfaces with lemon juice to keep them from discolouring.

2. Heat the oil in a heavy-based saucepan, add the onion and fry gently until soft and translucent. Add the chopped fennel leaves, the artichoke wedges, and 3 or 4 tablespoonsful of water. Season with salt and pepper to taste. Cover and cook over very low heat.

3. Meanwhile, shell the broad beans and the peas and rinse in cold water.

4. When the artichokes are half-cooked (after about 15 minutes, depending on the size and the freshness of the artichokes) add the broad beans, and the peas. Check that there is enough moisture in the pan to cook the vegetables, if in doubt, add 1 or 2 tablespoonsful of warm water. Cover the pan and simmer gently for 15-20 minutes more.

5. Adjust the seasoning. Serve at room temperature.

CAULIFLOWER RING
Cavolfiore in corona

(Serves 4 to 6)

Imperial (Metric)	American
1 large cauliflower	1 large cauliflower
(approx. 2-2½ lbs/1-1.2 kilos)	(approx. 2-2½ pounds)
Sea salt	Sea salt
1 quantity Béchamel Sauce	1 quantity Béchamel Sauce
(page 124)	(page 124)
4oz (100g) grated Parmesan	1 cupful grated Parmesan
cheese	cheese
3 eggs, beaten	3 eggs, beaten
¾ pint (425ml) Tomato Sauce	2 cupsful Tomato Sauce
(pages 129-131)	(pages 129-131)
Fresh basil leaves to garnish,	Fresh basil leaves to garnish,
when in season	when in season

1. Trim the cauliflower and divide into florets. Cook for 10-15 minutes in boiling salted water, then drain thoroughly. Mash the cauliflower or put it through a mouli-legumes, whichever you find easiest, and put in a bowl.

2. Prepare the *Salsa balsamella*. Remove pan from the heat and stir in the cauliflower and Parmesan cheese. Allow to cool slightly, then beat in the eggs. Mix well. Taste, and adjust seasoning if necessary.

3. Pour the mixture into a well-oiled 9inch (23cm) ring mould. Tap the mould lightly to settle the mixture, then smooth the surface. Bake in a preheated oven to 350°F/180°C (Gas Mark 4) for 35-40 minutes.

4. Remove from the oven, leave to stand for 5 minutes, then invert onto a warmed serving dish. Spoon the hot tomato sauce over and serve immediately.

STEWED PEPPERS WITH TOMATOES
Peperonata

(Serves 4)

Imperial (Metric)	American
4 large red peppers	4 large red peppers
4 tablespoonsful olive oil	4 tablespoonsful olive oil
½ lb (225g) onions, sliced	1½ cupsful sliced onions
2 cloves of garlic, peeled and sliced	2 cloves of garlic, peeled and sliced
2 small bay leaves	2 small bay leaves
1 lb (450g) fresh tomatoes, peeled, seeded and coarsely chopped	1 pound fresh tomatoes, peeled, seeded and coarsely chopped
Sea salt and freshly ground black pepper	Sea salt and freshly ground black pepper

1. Wash and dry the peppers. Cut them into halves lengthwise and remove stalks, seeds and white pith. Slice into long strips about ½ inch (1cm) wide.

2. Heat the oil in a large, heavy-based frying pan, add the onions, garlic and bay leaves and fry over a moderate heat until the onions soften and turn golden.

3. Add the peppers to the pan, reduce the heat, cover and cook for 10 minutes, stirring occasionally.

4. Add the tomatoes, and season to taste with a little salt and freshly ground black pepper; cook uncovered over a moderate heat, stirring from time to time, until most of the juices from the tomatoes has evaporated and the mixture is fairly thick.

5. Remove the bay leaves and adjust the seasoning if necessary. Serve the *Peperonata* hot as a vegetable dish, or cold as a side salad, or a starter.

GREEN BEANS WITH TOMATO SAUCE
Fagiolini verdi con salsa di pomodoro

(Serves 4 as a side dish)

Imperial (Metric)	American
1 lb (450g) green beans	1 pound string beans
1 lb (450g) ripe fresh tomatoes or 14 oz (400g) tin tomatoes, coarsely chopped with their juice	1 pound ripe fresh tomatoes or 1 medium can tomatoes, coarsely chopped with their juice
2 tablespoonsful olive oil	2 tablespoonsful olive oil
1 medium onion, chopped	1 medium onion, chopped
1 large clove of garlic, peeled and crushed	1 large clove of garlic, peeled and crushed
½ teaspoonful oregano	½ teaspoonful oregano
Sea salt and freshly ground black pepper	Sea salt and freshly ground black pepper

1. Wash, top, tail and remove strings from beans, if necessary. If using fresh tomatoes, blanch, peel and chop them.

2. Heat the oil in a saucepan and fry the onion until transparent. Add beans, tomatoes, garlic, oregano and seasoning to taste. Cover and simmer over a low heat for about 45 minutes, depending on the size and freshness of the beans. The beans should be tender, but firm and crisp to the bite, and the tomatoes reduced to a pulp. If necessary add 1 or 2 tablespoonsful of water during cooking to prevent sticking in the pan. Serve hot.

STUFFED ARTICHOKES SICILIAN STYLE
Carciofi imbottiti alla Siciliana

(Serves 4)

Imperial (Metric)	American
3 oz (75 g) fresh wholemeal breadcrumbs	1½ cupsful fresh wholewheat breadcrumbs
4 oz (100 g) freshly grated Parmesan or Pecorino cheese	1 cupful freshly grated Parmesan or Pecorino cheese
1 small onion, finely chopped	1 small onion, finely chopped
2 cloves of garlic, peeled and crushed	2 cloves of garlic, peeled and crushed
4 tablespoonsful finely chopped fresh parsley	4 tablespoonsful finely chopped fresh parsley
Sea salt and freshly ground black pepper	Sea salt and freshly ground black pepper
4 medium globe artichokes	4 medium globe artichokes
4 tablespoonsful olive oil	4 tablespoonsful olive oil
2-3 pieces of lemon rind	2-3 pieces of lemon rind

1. Mix together the breadcrumbs, cheese, onion, garlic, parsley, salt and pepper. Set aside.

2. Trim the stalks at the base of the artichokes. Remove any discoloured leaves and cut off about ½ inch (1 cm) from the tips of the artichoke leaves. Wash the artichokes in cold water and drain.

3. Spread the leaves apart and fill the spaces between them with the breadcrumb mixture, pressing it down firmly with the back of a metal spoon.

4. Place the stuffed artichokes in a heavy-based saucepan, just large enough to hold them upright. Pour 1 tablespoonsful of olive oil over the top of each artichoke. Fill with water half-way up the artichokes. Add ½ teaspoonful of sea salt and the pieces of lemon rind to the water.

5. Bring to the boil; reduce the heat, cover and simmer gently for 40 to 50 minutes, or until the outer leaves can be easily removed. Remove the artichokes from the water and serve hot or at room temperature.

9. Salads
Le insalate

A salad can be served as a starter, a main course, or after the main course as is common in Italy where it is considered a course in its own right. Vegetables in salads are used raw or cooked, alone or mixed and the composition changes with the seasons. One of my favourite winter salad vegetables is *radicchio,* or red chicory, with its tart taste. *Radicchio,* native of Treviso near Venice, is not easily found in this country, though it is becoming increasingly popular in good markets and can sometimes be found in an Italian grocery shop. It is well worth seeking out for its glorious colour, when available – use it in place of ordinary chicory. During the winter months when lettuce is expensive, raw young spinach leaves are widely used and make a nice change from lettuce. A frequent addition to an Italian salad is *arugula,* often known as garden rocket (*rucola* in Italian) a herb who's pungent flavour is much loved. Rocket, although difficult to find in greengrocers, is easy to grow in the garden and seeds are available from professional nurserymen. Used sparingly it adds an interesting bit to a salad.

A good olive oil is essential for salad dressings. Use green olive oil from the first pressing whenever possible. A first pressing olive oil is characterized by its low acidity – less than 1 per cent – which gives it a markedly fruity flavour.

ITALIAN MIXED SALAD
Insalata mista

(Serves 4)

Imperial (Metric)	American
1 Cos or Webbs lettuce	1 Cos or Webbs lettuce
1 fennel bulb	1 fennel bulb
½ small cucumber, sliced	½ small cucumber, sliced
6 radishes, trimmed and sliced	6 radishes, trimmed and sliced
1 celery heart, chopped	1 celery heart, chopped
1 small green pepper, cored, de-seeded and sliced	1 small green pepper, cored, de-seeded and sliced
4 spring onions, thinly sliced	4 scallions, thinly sliced
2 ripe, firm tomatoes	2 ripe, firm tomatoes
Sea salt	Sea salt
4 tablespoonsful olive oil	4 tablespoonsful olive oil
2 teaspoonsful cider vinegar or lemon juice	2 teaspoonsful cider vinegar or lemon juice

1. Pull off and discard any of the lettuce's bruised or blemished outer leaves. Wash and shake dry in a salad basket. Tear into bite-sized pieces and place in a salad bowl.

2. Trim the stalks, base and coarse outer leaves from the fennel, cut downwards into thin slices, then into strips. Add to the salad bowl with the cucumber, radishes, celery, pepper and spring onions (scallions).

3. Wipe the tomatoes, cut into quarters then in eighths and add to the bowl.

4. When ready to serve, sprinkle with a little salt and add the oil and the cider vinegar or lemon juice and toss lightly together. Serve immediately.

RICE SALAD
Insalata di riso

(Serves 4)

Imperial (Metric)	American
½ lb (225g) long grain brown rice	1 cupful long grain brown rice
1 pint (570ml) water	2½ cupsful water
Sea salt	Sea salt
3 fl oz (90ml) olive oil	⅓ cupful olive oil
1 tablespoonful cider or wine vinegar	1 tablespoonful cider or wine vinegar
1 clove of garlic, peeled and crushed	1 clove of garlic, peeled and crushed
Freshly ground black pepper	Freshly ground black pepper
½ cucumber, diced	½ cucumber, diced
4 spring onions, chopped	4 scallions, chopped
4 celery sticks, chopped	4 celery stalks, chopped
1 small green, red or yellow pepper, cored, de-seeded and thinly sliced	1 small green, red or yellow pepper, cored, de-seeded and thinly sliced
A few crisp lettuce leaves	A few crisp lettuce leaves
2 tablespoonsful chopped fresh parsley	2 tablespoonsful chopped fresh parsley

1. Put the rice into a large, heavy-based saucepan with the water. Add ½ teaspoonful salt and bring to the boil. Cover the pan, reduce the heat and simmer very gently for 40 minutes or until the rice is tender and all the water absorbed.

2. Mix together in a bowl the oil, vinegar, garlic, salt and some freshly-ground black pepper. Add the warm rice and mix everything lightly with a fork. Cover and leave until cold.

3. When ready to serve, add the chopped vegetables, mixing them in lightly. Taste and check the seasoning.

4. Line a shallow bowl with the lettuce, pile the rice salad in the centre and serve sprinkled with chopped parsley. Serve immediately.

SPINACH SALAD
Insalata di spinaci

(Serves 4)

Imperial (Metric)	American
4 slices wholemeal bread	4 slices wholewheat bread
1 oz (25g) butter or polyunsaturated margarine	2½ tablespoonsful butter or polyunsaturated margarine
3 fl oz (90ml) olive oil	⅓ cupful olive oil
1 clove of garlic	1 clove of garlic
½ lb (225g) young spinach leaves	8 ounces young spinach leaves
6 radishes, trimmed and sliced	6 radishes, trimmed and sliced
1 tablespoonful capers, rinsed	1 tablespoonful capers, rinsed
2 tablespoonsful red wine vinegar	2 tablespoonsful red wine vinegar
Sea salt and freshly ground black pepper	Sea salt and freshly ground black pepper
1 small onion, thinly sliced into rings	1 small onion, thinly sliced into rings

1. Remove the crusts from the bread and cut into large cubes. Fry in melted butter or margarine with 1 tablespoonful of oil, turning frequently until crisp and golden; drain croûtons on kitchen paper.

2. Lightly crush the clove of garlic and rub the inside of a salad bowl and discard.

3. Wash the spinach in several changes of cold water, drain. Tear the spinach into bite-sized pieces and add to the bowl with the croûtons, radishes and capers.

4. Add the remaining oil, the wine vinegar and a little seasoning. Toss thoroughly and arrange the onion rings on top. Serve immediately.

BEAN AND PEPPER SALAD
Insalata con i fagioli e peperoni

(Serves 4)

Imperial (Metric)	American
½ lb (225g) dried white beans of your choice, soaked overnight	1 cupful dried white beans of your choice, soaked overnight
1 clove of garlic	1 clove of garlic
2-3 fresh sage leaves	2-3 fresh sage leaves
1 small onion, finely chopped	1 small onion, finely chopped
1 celery stick, finely chopped	1 celery stalk, finely chopped
4 tablespoonsful olive oil	4 tablespoonsful olive oil
1 tablespoonful cider vinegar	1 tablespoonful cider vinegar
3 tablespoonsful lemon juice	3 tablespoonsful lemon juice
½ teaspoonful oregano	½ teaspoonful oregano
Sea salt and freshly ground black pepper	Sea salt and freshly ground black pepper
1 large yellow pepper	1 large yellow pepper
1 large green pepper	1 large green pepper
1 head chicory	1 head endive
1 tablespoonful chopped fresh parsley	1 tablespoonful chopped fresh parsley

1. Rinse the beans with cold water and then place them in a saucepan with the garlic clove and sage. Cover with plenty of water, bring to the boil and simmer gently for about 1½-2 hours, or until the beans are tender.

2. In a bowl mix together the chopped onion and celery with the oil, cider vinegar, lemon juice and oregano. Add seasoning to taste.

3. As soon as the beans are tender, drain them and toss them in the dressing while they are still warm. If possible leave the beans to marinate for several hours.

4. Wipe the peppers with a damp cloth and cut in half lengthwise. Remove the stalks, seeds and white pith. Cut into thin strips.

5. Separate the leaves from the chicory (endive). Wash and dry them. Put the larger leaves around the edge of a salad bowl with the greenish tips pointing upwards. Chop the remaining chicory (endive) and put it in the centre with the beans and chopped vegetables. Sprinkle with chopped parsley and serve.

ORANGE AND FENNEL SALAD
Insalata di arance e finocchi

(Serves 2-3 as a side dish)

Imperial (Metric)	American
1 large fennel bulb or 2 small ones	1 large fennel bulb or 2 small ones
3 oranges	3 oranges
1 small lemon	1 small lemon
2 tablespoonsful olive oil	2 tablespoonsful olive oil
Sea salt and freshly ground black pepper	Sea salt and freshly ground black pepper
8 black olives	8 black olives

1. Wash, trim and cut the fennel into thick wedges lengthwise.

2. Cut the tops and bottoms off the oranges. Hold them over a serving dish and cut away the peel and white pith with a small sharp or serrated knife, Slice thinly across the segments and arrange in a shallow serving dish with the fennel.

3. Cut off peel and pith from half of the lemon and chop the flesh. Sprinkle over the orange and fennel.

4. Pour over the olive oil and a little lemon juice from the reserved half lemon. Season with a little salt and a few twists of freshly ground black pepper.

5. Toss well. Cover and chill until required. Just before serving decorate with black olives.

Note: In Italy this is made with Sicilian oranges which have no pips.

POTATO SALAD
Insalata di patate

(Serves 4-6)

Imperial (Metric)	American
2 lbs (900g) waxy new potatoes	2 pounds waxy new potatoes
Sea salt	Sea salt
1 onion, sliced into rings	1 onion, sliced into rings
Freshly ground black pepper	Freshly ground black pepper
3 fl oz (90ml) olive oil	$\frac{1}{3}$ cupful olive oil
4 tablespoonsful cider vinegar or red wine vinegar	4 tablespoonsful cider vinegar or red wine vinegar
1 tablespoonful chopped fresh parsley	1 tablespoonful chopped fresh parsley

1. Scrub the potatoes and cook with their skins on in boiling salted water until just tender, about 15-20 minutes depending on size.

2. Drain. Remove the skins as soon as you can handle them. If small, keep whole, otherwise cut into ¼ inch (5mm) thick slices.

3. Place in a bowl, sprinkle with salt and pepper, add the onion and dress with olive oil and cider or wine vinegar, toss gently, being careful not to break up the potatoes too much. Garnish with chopped parsley and serve warm.

MIXED COOKED VEGETABLE SALAD
Insalatone

(Serves 4 to 6)

Imperial (Metric)	American
1 lb (450g) waxy potatoes	1 pound waxy potatoes
½ lb (225g) cauliflower cut into florets	8 ounces cauliflower cut into florets
Sea salt	Sea salt
4 oz (100g) green beans, topped and tailed	4 ounces green beans, topped and tailed
4 oz (100g) shelled peas	⅔ cupful shelled peas
3-4 medium onions	3-4 medium onions
Freshly ground black pepper	Freshly ground black pepper
4 tablespoonsful olive oil	¼ cupful olive oil
1 tablespoonful cider vinegar or red wine vinegar	1 tablespoonful cider vinegar or red wine vinegar
2 tablespoonsful fresh parsley, chopped	2 tablespoonsful fresh parsley, chopped

1. Scrub the potatoes and boil them with their skins on, until tender. Drain and cut into small chunks. Put them in a salad bowl.

2. In a second saucepan, cook the cauliflower florets in boiling salted water. Cut the beans into 1 inch (2.5 cm) lengths and add to pan with the peas. Simmer gently for 5-10 minutes till just tender. Drain. Add to the bowl.

3. Meanwhile, bake the onions whole, with their skins on, in a hot oven at 400°F/200°F (Gas Mark 6) until they are tender; about 1 hour. Peel the outer skin, then cut each one into quarters, and add to the salad bowl.

4. Pour the oil and cider or red wine vinegar over the vegetables while they are still hot. They will absorb the flavour of the dressing while they are cooling. Add the chopped parsley and toss lightly to mix. Serve immediately.

FENNEL AND CUCUMBER SALAD
Insalata di finocchi e cetrioli

(Serves 2 to 3)

Imperial (Metric)	American
½ small cucumber	½ small cucumber
3-4 radishes, sliced	3-4 radishes, sliced
1 large bulb Florence fennel	1 large bulb Florence fennel
1 clove of garlic, peeled and sliced	1 clove of garlic, peeled and sliced
1 teaspoonful fresh mint, chopped	1 teaspoonful fresh mint, chopped
Olive oil	Olive oil
Lemon juice	Lemon juice
Sea salt and freshly ground black pepper	Sea salt and freshly ground black pepper

1. Wash the cucumber, trim, slice thinly, and place in a bowl.

2. Trim the fennel and remove any bruised or discoloured parts, reserving any feathery leaves to sprinkle over the salad at the last minute. Cut the fennel in half lengthwise. Cut thin slices across each half, starting at stalk end. Put in a salad bowl with the cucumber and radishes.

3. In another bowl, mix together the mint, oil, lemon juice and seasoning to taste. Pour over salad and toss lightly. Sprinkle with fennel leaves and serve immediately.

MOZZARELLA AND TOMATO SALAD
Insalata di mozzarella e pomodoro

(Serves 3-4 as a side dish)

Imperial (Metric)	American
½ lb (225 g) fresh Mozzarella cheese	8 ounces fresh Mozzarella cheese
5 large tomatoes, sliced	5 large tomatoes, sliced
Olive oil	Olive oil
Sea salt and freshly ground black pepper	Sea salt and freshly ground black pepper
½ teaspoonful oregano, or fresh basil leaves, when in season	½ teaspoonful oregano, or fresh basil leaves, when in season

1. Thickly slice the cheese and place in the centre of a large flat serving plate. Arrange the tomato slices neatly around it.

2. Pour oil generously over the cheese and tomatoes and then season with salt and pepper. Sprinkle over the oregano or, when in season, garnish with fresh basil leaves.

TUSCAN BREAD AND VEGETABLE SALAD
Panzanella

(Serves 4 to 6)

Imperial (Metric)	American
1 large red onion	1 large red onion
8 thick slices almost stale wholemeal bread (preferably home-made)	8 thick slices almost stale wholewheat bread (preferably home-made)
10 fresh basil leaves, when in season	10 fresh basil leaves, when in season
½ cucumber, thinly sliced	½ cucumber, thinly sliced
4 large ripe tomatoes, cut into thick wedges	4 large ripe tomatoes, cut into thick wedges
8 green olives, stoned and halved	8 green olives, stoned and halved
2 tablespoonsful capers, rinsed	2 tablespoonsful capers, rinsed
1 small red pepper	1 small red pepper
1 small yellow pepper	1 small yellow pepper
⅓ pint (200ml) olive oil	¾ cupful olive oil
2 tablespoonsful cider vinegar	2 tablespoonsful cider vinegar
Sea salt and freshly ground black pepper	Sea salt and freshly ground black pepper

1. Peel and thinly slice the onion and separate into rings. The onion should be soaked in two or more changes of cold water for at least ½ hour before putting it in the salad. This helps to sweeten it.

2. Remove the crusts and soak the bread in enough cold water to cover it, then squeeze out the excess moisture. Put into a bowl, mash with a fork to obtain a crumbly consistency, and mix in the coarsely chopped basil leaves, the sliced cucumber, the tomatoes and the olives and capers.

3. Cut each pepper in half lengthwise, remove stalks, seeds and white pith. Cut the peppers into thin strips and add to the salad.

4. Add the pre-soaked onion slices. Then stir in the olive oil, cider vinegar and a little salt and pepper, blend thoroughly with a fork. Chill the salad for at least 30 minutes before serving, so that the bread and vegetables can absorb the dressing. Just enough dressing should be added so that the bread is moist, but not soggy.

10. Sauces

The most important sauces in the Italian kitchen are those used for pasta, and there is an infinite variety of them. But, for the Italian cook, they do not have an independent existence of their own; they are simply extensions of the dish in which they appear. For this reason, many of the recipes for sauces are given with the dishes to which they are particularly well suited, in other sections of the book.

BÉCHAMEL SAUCE
Salsa balsamella

(Makes about ¾ pint/425ml/2 cupsful)

This classic sauce, which is also known in Italy as *Salsa besciamella*, was used in Italian cooking long before it made its appearance in France. These quantities make a medium-thick sauce which is right for most of the dishes mentioned in the other sections in this book. It can be made thicker or thinner by using less or more milk.

Imperial (Metric)
¾ pint (425ml) milk
2 oz (50g) butter
1½ oz (40g) plain wholemeal flour
Freshly grated nutmeg
Sea salt and freshly ground black pepper
Bay leaf (optional)

American
2 cupsful milk
¼ cupful butter
⅓ cupful wholewheat flour
Freshly grated nutmeg
Sea salt and freshly ground black pepper
Bay leaf (optional)

1. In a small saucepan, heat the milk until it comes to the very edge of the boil.

2. Melt the butter over a low heat in a heavy-based saucepan. When it bubbles, but before it starts to turn brown, add the flour and cook, stirring, for 2 minutes to form a smooth, glossy paste.

3. Turn off the heat and add the milk, a little at a time, stirring vigorously with a wooden spoon as you pour, so that it is absorbed by the flour; continue adding it gradually until it is all incorporated.

4. When this has been done, return the pan to the heat, turned to its lowest possible setting, and cook the sauce for 10 to 15 minutes or until thickened and smooth. Season with salt, pepper and freshly grated nutmeg to taste. Use sauce as required. If you are not using the sauce immediately, float flakes of butter on top, or cover with a piece of cling film, to prevent a skin from forming.

Note: For additional flavour, add a bay leaf to the milk before heating. Remove before adding the milk to the sauce.

GENOESE BASIL SAUCE
Pesto alla Genovese

(Makes enough for 4 servings of pasta)

This is the famous sauce which is eaten by the Genoese with all kinds of pasta, with gnocchi, and as a flavouring for soups. *Pesto* is traditionally made in a mortar and pestle (from which it gets its name) but nowadays every Italian cook seems to use a blender or food processor, which makes it in a fraction of the time. It does, however, require fresh basil, and there is no substitute. I know the difficulty in obtaining fresh basil in the large quantities needed for this sauce, so in order to make it you will probably have to grow the basil yourself. I find that basil grows quite well in pots on a sunny window-sill.

The old, traditional recipes do not mention pine nuts, but modern *pesto* invariably includes them, and so does this recipe. If pine nuts are not available substitute walnut pieces. Parmesan and Pecorino Sardo cheese are sometimes used in equal quantities, or all Parmesan which gives the *pesto* a milder flavour.

Pesto freezes well if you leave out the cheese and add it when thawed, and will also keep in the refrigerator for 2-3 weeks in a tightly-closed jar.

Imperial (Metric)	American
2 oz (50g) fresh basil leaves, weighed after stripping from the stalks	2 packed cupsful fresh basil leaves, measured. after stripping from the stalks
¼ teaspoonful sea salt	¼ teaspoonful sea salt
2-3 cloves of garlic, peeled and crushed	2-3 cloves of garlic, peeled and crushed
3 fl oz (90ml) olive oil	⅓ cupful olive oil
1 tablespoonful pine nuts	1 tablespoonful pine kernels
2 oz (50g) freshly grated Parmesan or Sardo cheese, mixed together in equal quantities	½ cupful freshly grated Parmesan or Sardo cheese, mixed together in equal quantities

Two recipes are given here, one for the blender or food processor, the other for a mortar and pestle.

Pesto made in the blender:
1. Put the basil, olive oil, pine nuts, garlic and salt in a blender or food-

processor and blend until you have a smooth purée. (Freeze at this stage if required.)

2. Transfer the purée to a bowl and stir in the cheese.

Pesto made in a mortar and pestle:

1. In a large mortar, grind the garlic, pine nuts and salt to a pulp.

2. Tear the basil leaves and pound them into a paste – alternating between pounding and turning with a grinding motion. Add the grated cheese and a trickle of oil and continue to grind with the pestle until the mixture is thoroughly blended.

3. Add more oil in a slow trickle; stir the sauce with the pestle until the sauce is smooth and creamy.

Note: In Italy the *pesto* is thinned by adding to it 2-3 tablespoonsful of the hot water in which the pasta is cooked.

MAYONNAISE
Maionese

(Makes ½ pint/285ml/1⅓ cupsful)

Make sure all the ingredients are at room temperature. To help you add the oil slowly, place the measured quantity in a small-necked bottle fitted with a cork in which a groove has been cut. Mayonnaise can take up to 20 minutes to make, but it should be a very satisfying process. It is very important that you do not rush through it.

Imperial (Metric)	American
2 large egg yolks	2 large egg yolks
1 level teaspoonful sea salt	1 level teaspoonful sea salt
Freshly ground black pepper	Freshly ground black pepper
⅓ pint (200ml) olive oil	¾ cupful olive oil
2 teaspoonsful lemon juice or white wine vinegar	2 teaspoonsful lemon juice or white wine vinegar

1. Put the egg yolks into a medium-sized bowl, add the salt and a few twists of freshly ground black pepper and whisk (with an electric hand-whisk or a balloon whisk) until very pale and the consistency of thick cream.

2. Add the oil drop by drop, whisking well between additions. Once the emulsion starts thickening, you can begin adding bigger drops.

3. When about half the oil is in, you can add a few drops of the lemon juice or vinegar; this will make the mixture thinner, and at this point you can start pouring in the oil in a thin, steady trickle (whisking all the time) until all the oil has been absorbed, thinning the emulsion with the remainder of the lemon juice or vinegar as needed.

4. The finished mayonnaise should be smooth, glossy and the consistency of thick cream. Taste and adjust the seasoning.

Note: If the mayonnaise curdles (and this will happen if the oil is added too quickly at the beginning) don't panic. Place a fresh egg yolk into a clean bowl, add the curdled mixture to this, again drop by drop, then carry on with the remainder of the oil. The finished mayonnaise may be thicker, so whisk in a little extra oil until the required consistency is reached. Store the mayonnaise in a screw-top jar in a cool place – such as the bottom shelf of the refrigerator – for no longer than a week.

TOMATO SAUCE I
Salsa di pomodoro

(Makes ¾ pint/425ml/2 cupsful)

Imperial (Metric)	American
1½ lbs (675g) ripe tomatoes	1½ pounds ripe tomatoes
2 tablespoonsful olive oil	2 tablespoonsful olive oil
1 clove of garlic, peeled and crushed	1 clove of garlic, peeled and crushed
2 level teaspoonsful tomato purée	2 level teaspoonsful tomato paste
1 tablespoonful fresh basil, chopped, or 1 tablespoonful dried basil	1 tablespoonful fresh basil, chopped, or 1 teaspoonful dried basil
Sea salt and freshly ground black pepper	Sea salt and freshly ground black pepper

1. Scald the tomatoes in boiling water, leave for 2-3 minutes, then drain and peel away the skins. Halve and remove their fibrous cores, then chop the flesh quite small.

2. Heat the oil in a heavy-based saucepan, add the onion and the garlic and fry until they are soft but not brown. Add the tomatoes, tomato purée, the dried basil and salt and pepper to taste. (If using fresh basil, add it just before serving.)

3. Simmer the sauce, partially covered, for 30-40 minutes. This will allow some of the excess liquid to reduce, and concentrate the flavour. Taste and adjust the seasoning. Then purée in a blender or push through a sieve — or if you like, serve it just as it is.

TOMATO SAUCE II
Salsa di pomodoro

(Makes 1 pint/570ml/2½ cupsful)

Imperial (Metric)	American
2 tablespoonsful olive oil	2 tablespoonsful olive oil
1 medium onion, finely chopped	1 medium onion, finely chopped
1 celery stick, finely chopped	1 celery stalk, finely chopped
2 x 14oz (400g) tins tomatoes or 2lbs (900g) fresh, ripe tomatoes	2 medium cans tomatoes or 2 pounds fresh, ripe tomatoes
1 bay leaf	1 bay leaf
Sprig of thyme or rosemary	Sprig of thyme or rosemary
2 or 3 sprigs parsley	2 or 3 sprigs parsley
Sprig of basil (optional)	Sprig of basil (optional)
½ teaspoonful raw cane sugar	½ teaspoonful raw cane sugar
Seasoning to taste	Seasoning to taste

1. Heat the oil in a heavy-based saucepan. Add the onion and celery and fry over low heat for 5 minutes, stirring frequently, until they have softened but are not coloured.

2. Add the tomatoes, together with their juice if you are using tinned ones, peeled and coarsely chopped if they are fresh. Add the remaining ingredients, then cover and simmer very gently for 45 minutes to 1 hour, or until the sauce has reduced to a thickish consistency. Stir sauce often to prevent burning.

3. Put through a sieve or a fine mouli-legumes, taste and adjust the seasoning, and, if the sauce is to be used at once, return to the pan to reheat.

TOMATO SAUCE III
Salsa di pomodoro

(Makes about ½ pint/275ml/1⅓ cupsful)

Imperial (Metric)	American
14 oz (400g) tin peeled plum tomatoes	1 medium can peeled plum tomatoes
1 medium onion, finely chopped	1 medium onion, finely chopped
1 carrot, finely chopped	1 carrot, finely chopped
1 celery stick, finely chopped	1 celery stalk, finely chopped
2 teaspoonsful tomato purée	2 teaspoonsful tomato paste
½ teaspoonful raw cane sugar (optional)	½ teaspoonful raw cane sugar (optional)
Sea salt and freshly ground black pepper	Sea salt and freshly ground black pepper
3 tablespoonsful olive oil	3 tablespoonsful olive oil
2 teaspoonsful fresh basil, finely chopped, or 1 teaspoonful dried basil (optional)	2 teaspoonsful fresh basil, finely chopped, or 1 teaspoonful dried basil (optional)

1. Put the tomatoes with their juice, the onion, celery, carrot, tomato purée and sugar (if using) into a saucepan. Add a little salt and pepper and stir with a wooden spoon to break up the tomatoes. Bring to the boil, reduce the heat and simmer, partially covered, for 30 minutes.

2. Press the sauce through a sieve or purée it in a blender, return to the pan, add the olive oil, and simmer, uncovered, for 15 minutes. Check the seasoning and stir in the basil, if using.

Variation: Fry the chopped vegetables in the oil until soft but not brown before adding the other ingredients.

11. Ices
I gelati

Genuine Italian ices – *gelati* and *granite* are becoming scarce nowadays even in Italy, but we can recreate at home the true flavour of these desserts by using wholesome natural ingredients.

HAZELNUT ICE-CREAM
Gelato alla nocciola

(Serves 4 to 6)

Imperial (Metric)	American
4 oz (100g) hazelnuts (shelled weight)	¾ cupful hazelnut kernels
4 egg yolks	4 egg yolks
3 oz (75g) light Muscovado sugar	½ cupful light Muscovado sugar
½ pint (275ml) milk	1⅓ cupsful milk
½ pint (275ml) double cream	1⅓ cupsful heavy cream

1. Spread the nuts on a baking sheet and place under a preheated moderate grill, shaking frequently, until the skins split. Tip into a rough towel and rub off the loose skins. Grind coarsely.

2. Put the egg yolks into a medium-sized bowl, add the sugar and beat (with an electric hand-whisk or a rotary whisk) until the mixture is pale, thick and creamy.

3. Heat the milk until it is just about to boil and pour over the egg mixture in a steady stream, whisking all the time.

4. Place the bowl over a pan of simmering water (or use a double saucepan) and cook, stirring, until the custard begins to thicken and coats the back of the spoon, but do not let it boil or it will curdle. Take off the heat. Stir in the ground nuts and set aside to cool.

5. Meanwhile, whip the cream until it just begins to thicken and fold into the cooled custard mixture. Pour into a freezerproof container, cover and freeze. As it hardens, push the sides of the mixture to the middle. When the mixture is nearly set, turn it out into a bowl and beat thoroughly. Then return to the freezer covered and leave until frozen.

6. Transfer to the refrigerator 1 hour before serving to soften.

STRAWBERRY GRANITA
Granita di fragole

(Serves 4 to 6)

Imperial (Metric)	American
1 1/4 lbs (550g) strawberries – to make 1 pint (570ml) of pulp	5 cupsful strawberries – to make 2 1/2 cupsful of pulp
5 oz (150g) honey	1/2 cupful honey
1/2 pint (275ml) water	1 1/3 cupsful water
1 1/2 tablespoonsful lemon juice	1 1/2 tablespoonsful lemon juice

1. Purée the strawberries in a blender or press them through a sieve.

2. Place the honey and water in a saucepan over moderate heat and stir until dissolved. Bring to the boil and continue to boil for 5 minutes. Cool to room temperature then stir in the puréed strawberries and lemon juice.

3. Pour the mixture into a shallow freezing tray. Stir the *granita* every 30 minutes and scrape into it the ice particles that form around the edges of the tray. The finished *granita* should have a snowy, granular texture. Spoon into tall glasses and serve immediately with a spoon.

Note: For a coarser texture pour the mixture into ice-cube trays and freeze the *granita* solid. Then remove the cubes and crush them in an ice crusher.

Variation: This method can also be used for making raspberry or blackberry *granita.*

LEMON SORBET
Sorbetto al limone

(Serves 4 to 6)

Imperial (Metric)	American
Pared rind and juice of 3 large lemons – to make ¼ pint (150ml) juice	Pared rind and juice of 3 large lemons – to make ⅔ cupful juice
6 oz (175g) honey	½ cupful honey
1 pint (570ml) water	2½ cupsful water
1 large egg white	1 large egg white

1. Put the pared lemon rind in a saucepan with the honey and water. Bring to the boil, stirring to dissolve the honey. Boil briskly for five minutes. Leave to cool, strain and add the lemon juice. Pour into ice-cube trays from which the dividers have been removed.

2. Freeze until mushy. Stir the ice crystals that form around the edge into the middle. Continue stirring every 30 minutes for about 3-4 hours.

3. Remove from the freezer and whisk until smooth. Beat up the egg white until stiff but not dry, then fold this into the whisked lemon mixture and return to the freezer covered, for a further 2-3 hours until it is the consistency of firm snow, at which point it is ready to serve.

STUFFED FROZEN ORANGES
Arance imbottiti

(Serves 6)

Imperial (Metric)	American
6 oranges	6 oranges
6 oz (175g) honey	½ cupful honey
1 teaspoonful finely grated lemon rind	1 teaspoonful finely grated lemon rind
1 teaspoonful finely grated orange rind	1 teaspoonful finely grated orange rind
¾ pint (425 ml) water	2 cupsful water
Juice of 1 lemon	Juice of 1 lemon
1 large egg white	1 large egg white
Fresh mint sprigs to decorate	Fresh mint sprigs to decorate

1. Neatly slice off the tops and scoop out the flesh of the oranges with a grapefruit knife. Use the flesh to make your sorbet to stuff the oranges (6 oranges and the juice of 1 lemon should yield about 1 pint/570ml/2½ cupsful of juice).

2. Put the hollowed-out shells and their tops into the freezer for about 4 hours, or keep in the freezer for as long as necessary until you are ready to use them.

3. Dissolve the honey in the water. Add the lemon and orange rind and boil for 5 minutes. Allow to cool, then strain the syrup into the orange and lemon juices. Pour into ice-cube trays with divisions removed. Freeze until mushy (see Lemon Sorbet recipe on page 134).

4. Remove from the freezer and beat until smooth. Add the stiffly beaten egg white and return to the freezer for a further 2-3 hours (taking it out a couple of times and stirring it to maintain the texture during that time).

5. When the sorbet is frozen, fill the orange shells, pressing the sorbet well down with the back of a metal spoon. Replace the lid. Wrap and return to the freezer.

6. Just before serving, remove the lid and place one or two mint leaves on the sorbet, with their tips draped over the edge of the orange rind. Replace the tops over the shells, at a slight angle, and serve.

ICED RASPBERRY MOUSSE
Spumoni di lamponi

(Serves 6 to 8)

Imperial (Metric)	American
2 lbs (900g) raspberries	2 pounds raspberries
4 tablespoonsful water	4 tablespoonsful water
4 oz (100g) honey	⅓ cupful honey
Juice of 1 lemon	Juice of 1 lemon
6 egg yolks	6 egg yolks
4 oz (100g) light Muscovado sugar	⅔ cupful light Muscovado sugar
Grated rind of 1 lemon	Grated rind of 1 lemon
¼ pint (150ml) water	⅔ cupful water
¾ pint (425ml) double cream	2 cupsful heavy cream

1. Reserve a few raspberries for decoration. Rub the remainder through a sieve with the honey, water and the lemon juice to form a purée.

2. Beat the egg yolks (with an electric hand-whisk or a rotary whisk) until pale, thick and creamy. Boil the sugar, lemon rind and the water together in a small saucepan for five minutes or until the syrup reads 230°F/110°C on a sugar thermometer. Pour the syrup over the egg yolks in a steady stream, beating all the time, and continue to beat until cool. Gradually stir in the raspberry purée.

3. Whip the cream until it just begins to thicken, and fold into the raspberry mixture.

4. Whisk egg whites until just stiff and fold in. Pour into a mould. Chill and freeze. Turn out, decorate with reserved raspberries and serve with whipped cream.

12. Desserts, Cakes and Biscuits

On the whole, Italians are likely to finish lunch or dinner with fruit, cheese and wine. If they do have dessert, it will probably be something quite simple like fresh fruit salad or, perhaps, Zabaglione.

I have included in this section a collection of traditional cakes and desserts, many of which are delicacies that Italians would not do without on holidays and special occasions. Some of these are regional dishes and, like most Italian recipes, have been passed down from mother to daughter. It is these recipes that are my favourites, because they are part of the old traditional customs and yet are still enjoyed today.

FRUIT BREAD
Panettone

The Milanese *panettone* is a rich yeast cake containing candied fruit. Traditionally, it is eaten at Christmas, but nowadays *panettone* is often served with coffee throughout the year.

Imperial (Metric)	American
1 oz (25g) fresh yeast or ½ oz (15g) dried yeast	2½ tablespoonsful fresh yeast or 1 tablespoonful dried yeast
3 oz (75g) raw cane sugar	½ cupful raw cane sugar
4 tablespoonsful warm milk	4 tablespoonsful warm milk
3 beaten eggs – at room temperature	3 beaten eggs – at room temperature
1 teaspoonful vanilla essence	1 teaspoonful vanilla extract
2 teaspoonsful grated lemon rind	2 teaspoonsful grated lemon rind
Pinch of sea salt	Pinch of sea salt
¾ lb (350g) plain wholemeal flour	3 cupsful plain wholewheat flour
4 oz (100g) butter, softened	½ cupful butter, softened
3 oz (75g) sultanas, rinsed and drained	½ cupful golden seedless raisins, rinsed and drained
4 oz (100g) candied lemon peel, finely diced	⅔ cupful candied lemon peel, finely diced

To glaze:

1 egg yolk or 2 tablespoonsful milk	1 egg yolk or 2 tablespoonsful milk

1. Crumble the fresh yeast or sprinkle the dried yeast and a teaspoonful of the sugar into the warm milk and leave until frothy (about 10 minutes).

2. Put the yeast mixture into a large bowl. Mix with the eggs, vanilla, lemon rind, salt and the remaining sugar. Stir in enough flour (roughly ⅔) until the mixture is soft and sticky, but can just be gathered into a ball. Knead in the softened butter. Add the remainder of the flour, a little at a time, until the dough is soft, and firm. When it is no longer sticky, turn out onto a lightly floured surface and knead for 10 minutes, or until smooth and shiny.

3. Place the dough in a large, clean bowl. Cover. Leave in a warm place to double in size (about 1½ hours).

4. When risen, punch down and gently work in the sultanas (golden seedless raisins) and the lemon peel, a small amount at a time. Knead until fruit is evenly distributed.

5. Shape it into a ball. Place on a greased baking sheet and mark a cross on top. Tie a double collar of greaseproof paper around the dough, and leave in a warm place to rise again until double in size. The collar should measure about 8 inches (20cm) across. In Italy the *panettone* is baked in a special paper case called a *pirottino*.

6. Glaze the top with egg yolk or milk and bake in a preheated hot oven, 400°F/200°C (Gas Mark 6) for 10 minutes. Then reduce the heat to 350°F/180°C (Gas Mark 4) for a further 45 minutes or until well risen, golden brown and firm to the touch. Cool on a wire rack. To serve, cut the *panettone* into thick wedges.

ROMAN CHEESECAKE
Crostata di ricotta

(Serves 8)

For the pastry:

Imperial (Metric)	American
½ lb (225g) plain wholemeal flour	2 cupsful plain wholewheat flour
4 oz (100g) butter or polyunsaturated margarine	½ cupful butter or polyunsaturated margarine
2 egg yolks	2 egg yolks
1 oz (25g) raw cane sugar	2 tablespoonsful raw cane sugar
½ teaspoonful grated lemon rind	½ teaspoonful grated lemon rind
A pinch of sea salt	A pinch of sea salt
2 tablespoonsful Marsala	2 tablespoonsful Marsala

For the filling:

Imperial (Metric)	American
1½ lbs (675g) Ricotta or curd cheese rubbed through a sieve, mixed with 3 tablespoonsful double cream	1½ pounds Ricotta or curd cheese rubbed through a sieve, mixed with 3 tablespoonsful heavy cream
2 eggs, beaten	2 eggs, beaten
1 teaspoonful pure vanilla essence	1 teaspoonful pure vanilla extract
4 oz (100g) raw cane sugar	⅔ cupful raw cane sugar
4 tablespoonsful plain wholemeal flour	¼ cupful plain wholewheat flour
1 oz (25g) sultanas, rinsed and drained	3 tablespoonsful golden seedless raisins, rinsed and drained
2 tablespoonsful candied peel, finely diced (optional)	2 tablespoonsful candied peel, finely diced (optional)

To glaze:

1 egg white, beaten with 2 teaspoonsful of water, to glaze	1 egg white, beaten with 2 teaspoonsful of water, to glaze

1. Proceed as for *Pasta frolla* (page 158) with the above pastry ingredients. Wrap in greaseproof paper and chill. Prepare the filling.

2. Put the Ricotta or curd cheese, eggs, vanilla essence and sugar together in a mixing bowl, and beat until they are thoroughly mixed.

Fold in the sifted flour and then stir in the sultanas (golden seedless raisins) and peel, if used.

3. Roll out the pastry thinly to line a 9 inches (23cm) loose-bottomed flan tin. If you should find that the pastry is sticky, roll out between two sheets of greaseproof (wax) paper. Trim off the excess and cut into long thin strips.

4. Fill the pastry case with the cheese mixture, spreading it evenly with a spatula, then arrange the extra pieces of pastry in a lattice design on top. Brush the strips with the egg white and water mixture.

5. Bake in the centre of a preheated moderate oven, 350°F/180°F (Gas Mark 4) for about 1 hour, until the crust is golden and the filling is firm. Turn off the heat, open the oven door and leave the cheesecake there for about an hour. It should be quite cold before cutting.

Note: Ricotta and curd cheese can be on the wet side; if it is, wrap it in muslin and press out the moisture overnight. Too much moisture can upset the texture.

SICILIAN CAKE
Cassata alla Siciliana

(Serves 8)

For the cake:

Imperial (Metric)	American
4 eggs	4 eggs
4 oz (100g) raw cane sugar	⅔ cupful raw cane sugar
½ teaspoonful pure vanilla essence	½ teaspoonful pure vanilla extract
4 oz (100g) 81 or 100% plain wholemeal flour	1 cupful 81 or 100% plain wholewheat flour

For the filling:

Imperial (Metric)	American
1 lb (450g) fresh Ricotta or curd cheese	2 cupsful fresh Ricotta or curd cheese
3 tablespoonsful raw cane sugar	3 tablespoonsful raw cane sugar
3 fl oz (90ml) Marsala or sweet sherry	⅓ cupful Marsala or sweet sherry
1 oz (25g) shelled pistachio nuts, chopped or chopped walnuts	¼ cupful shelled pistachio nuts, chopped or chopped English walnuts
2 oz (50g) block carob, coarsely chopped	⅓ cupful coarsely chopped block carob
2 oz (50g) candied peel, chopped	⅓ cupful chopped candied peel

For the topping:

Imperial (Metric)	American
4 oz (100g) block carob, broken into large chunks	⅔ cupful block carob, broken into large chunks
1 oz (25g) butter	2½ tablespoonsful butter
Candied peel	Candied peel

1. Beat the eggs, sugar and vanilla essence together, using either an electric or hand whisk, until very pale; the mixture should leave a definite trail from the whisk when you lift it out. Fold in the flour with a metal spoon.

2. Pour the mixture into two lined and greased 8 inch (20 cm) sandwich tins. Bake in an oven preheated to 400°F/200°C (Gas Mark 6) for 15 to 20 minutes until well risen, golden brown and springy to the touch. Turn onto a wire rack to cool.

3. Meanwhile prepare the filling. Beat the cheese and sugar together until smooth and light – the consistency of whipped cream. Add 2 tablespoonsful of Marsala. Fold in the chopped peel, nuts and carob. Mix well.

4. Cut both of the sponges horizontally in half. Place one portion of sponge on a flat plate, sprinkle with 1 tablespoonful Marsala and spread with ⅓ of the filling; repeat until all the sponge, Marsala and filling have been used up, ending with a plain layer of sponge on top.

5. Prepare the topping. Place 2-3 tablespoonsful of water and the carob chunks in a small saucepan over a gentle heat, and stir until the carob is melted. Take off the heat and beat in the butter until the mixture is creamy and glossy. Allow to cool slightly, then spread over the top of the cake. Decorate with candied peel.

6. Refrigerate the *cassata* for at least 2 hours before serving to let the flavours mingle.

POLENTA CAKE
Torta di polenta

(Serves 6 to 8)

This cake, made from maize (corn) meal, is a speciality from the Veneto region. It is traditionally served on New Year's Eve and is called *Pinza Veneta* by the Venetians.

Imperial (Metric)	American
1 pint (570ml) water	2½ cupsful water
½ teaspoonful sea salt	½ teaspoonful sea salt
½ lb (225g) fine maize meal	1½ cupsful fine corn meal
3 oz (75g) raw cane sugar	½ cupful raw cane sugar
2 oz (50g) raisins	⅓ cupful raisins
4 oz (100g) dried figs, chopped	¾ cupful chopped dried figs
2 oz (50g) candied peel, finely diced	⅓ cupful candied peel, finely diced
1 oz (25g) pine nuts	¼ cupful pine kernels
1½ oz (40g) butter or polyunsaturated margarine	3 tablespoonsful butter or polyunsaturated margarine
1 egg, well beaten	1 egg, well beaten
2 tablespoonsful Marsala (optional)	2 tablespoonsful Marsala (optional)
4 oz (100g) wholemeal flour	1 cupful plain wholewheat flour
Corn oil	Corn oil

1. Put the water into a medium-sized, heavy-based saucepan with the salt and bring to the boil. Sprinkle in the maize meal slowly, stirring vigorously as you do, so that it doesn't become lumpy. Reduce the heat and simmer gently, stirring and beating frequently with a wooden spoon. This mixture will become very thick.

2. When the *polenta* has cooked for 20 minutes remove the pan from the heat. Stir in the sugar, raisins, figs, candied peel, pine nuts (kernels) butter or margarine, egg, the Marsala (if used) and the flour; stirring thoroughly so that they are evenly distributed throughout the *polenta.*

3. Brush the sides and bottom of a 9 inch (23cm) round cake tin with corn oil. Spoon the mixture into the tin, levelling it off with a dampened spatula. Bake in a preheated moderately hot oven, 375°F/ 190°C (Gas Mark 5), for 40 to 50 minutes. Allow the cake to cool slightly before turning it out of the tin onto a wire rack to cool completely.

HAZELNUT BISCUITS
Biscotti alla nocciola

(Makes about 24)

Imperial (Metric)	American
6 oz (175g) shelled whole hazelnuts	1⅓ cupsful hazelnut kernels
4 oz (100g) butter or polyunsaturated margarine	½ cupful butter or polyunsaturated margarine
2 oz (50g) raw cane sugar	⅓ cupful raw cane sugar
4 oz (100g) honey	⅓ cupful honey
½ teaspoonful ground cinnamon	½ teaspoonful ground cinnamon
2 eggs, lightly beaten	2 eggs, lightly beaten
½ lb (225g) 81 or 100% self-raising wholemeal flour	2 cupsful 81 or 100% self-raising wholewheat flour
¼ teaspoonful sea salt	¼ teaspoonful sea salt

1. Spread the hazelnuts on a baking sheet and place under a preheated moderate grill until the skins split, shaking frequently. Turn into a tea towel and rub off the loose skins. Set aside.

2. Cream the butter or margarine, sugar and honey together until the mixture is light and fluffy. Add the ground cinnamon and then the beaten eggs, a little at a time. Stir in the flour and the salt. Add the toasted hazelnuts and fold them into the mixture until they are evenly incorporated.

3. Lay a sheet of greaseproof (wax) paper on a baking sheet and spoon the mixture on making two strips; they should measure about 9 inches (23cm) in length and 3½ inches (9cm) in width. Smooth the tops and even out the sides of the strips with a flexible spatula dipped in cold water.

4. Bake in a preheated oven, 375°F/190°C (Gas Mark 5) for 15-20 minutes, until they are pale golden and firm. Leave the strips to cool on a wire rack, and then peel them off the greaseproof wax paper.

5. With a sharp, serrated knife, cut across the strips to make slices about ¾ inch (2cm) wide and lay them flat, close together on the baking sheet. Dry them out in a preheated oven, 300°F/150°F (Gas Mark 2) for 10 minutes. Turn the biscuits over and bake the other side for 10 minutes or until crisp. Cool on a wire rack. If the biscuits are stored in an airtight tin, they will keep for about a month.

RICE CAKE
Torta di riso

(Serves 8)

Imperial (Metric)	American
1¾ pints (1 litre) milk or half milk and water	4½ cupsful milk or half milk and water
5 oz (150g) raw cane sugar	¾ cupful raw cane sugar
Grated rind of 1 lemon	Grated rind of 1 lemon
¾ lb (350g) short-grain brown rice	1½ cupsful short-grain brown rice
Sea salt	Sea salt
4 eggs, separated	4 eggs, separated
4 oz (100g) candied peel, chopped	⅔ cupful candied peel, chopped
2 oz (50g) raisins, washed and drained	⅓ cupful raisins, washed and drained
2 tablespoonsful rum (optional)	2 tablespoonsful rum (optional)
A knob of butter	A knob of butter
2 tablespoonsfuls fine dry wholemeal breadcrumbs	2 tablespoonsful fine dry wholewheat breadcrumbs

1. Heat the milk in a saucepan together with the sugar and grated lemon rind. When it comes to the boil add the rice and a pinch of salt. Reduce the heat and simmer gently, uncovered, for 2½ hours, or until the rice has absorbed all the milk. Remove from the heat and allow to cool.

2. Beat the egg yolks into the rice with a wooden spoon. Add the candied peel, raisins and the rum (if used). Mix all the ingredients thoroughly. Beat the egg whites until they form stiff peaks, then fold them into the mixture.

3. Smear the bottom and sides of a round 9 inch (23cm) spring-release cake tin with butter, sprinkle with breadcrumbs and shake off excess crumbs. Pour the mixture into the tin and bake in the middle of a preheated oven at 350°F/180°C (Gas Mark 4) for 1 hour.

Note: This cake improves with keeping and is best eaten 24 hours after it has been made.

HONEY BALLS
Struffoli

Imperial (Metric)	American
½ lb (225g) plain wholemeal flour	2 cupsful plain wholewheat flour
2 tablespoonsful raw cane sugar	2 tablespoonsful raw cane sugar
A pinch of sea salt	A pinch of sea salt
1 oz (25g) butter, softened	2½ tablespoonsful butter,
3 eggs	softened
1 teaspoonful pure vanilla	3 eggs
essence	1 teaspoonful pure vanilla
Corn oil for deep frying	extract
6 oz (175g) honey	Corn oil for deep frying
	½ cupful honey

1. Mix together the flour, sugar and salt. Make a well in the centre and put in the butter, eggs and vanilla essence. Gradually work the flour into the eggs until a smooth dough is obtained. Knead lightly on a floured board. Form into a ball. Cover with a tea towel and leave to rest for 30 minutes.

2. With floured hands, take small amounts of the dough and roll out into long rolls about ½ inch (1 cm) thick. Then cut into ¼ inch (5 mm) lengths.

3. Heat oil in a deep fryer to 350°F (180°C). Fry in batches, by dropping them in a few at a time and cooking for about 3 minutes, until puffed up and golden. Do not crowd pan. Continue until all the pieces have been fried. Drain on absorbent kitchen paper.

4. Put the honey into a saucepan and heat until it is liquid. Add the balls. Mix well over low heat for 2-3 minutes (no longer or honey will caramelize) so that they are evenly coated. Transfer to a large plate and arrange them into the shape of a ring. Serve after a few hours.

SIENA CAKE
Panforte di Siena

(Serves 8 to 10)

This round flat 'cake', consisting largely of almonds, hazelnuts and candied peel, is a speciality of the town of Siena.

Imperial (Metric)	American
4 oz (100g) shelled, blanched, coarsely chopped and roasted almonds	¾ cupful shelled, blanched, coarsely chopped and roasted almonds
4 oz (100g) shelled, coarsely chopped and roasted hazelnuts	¾ cupful shelled, coarsely chopped and roasted hazelnuts
6 oz (175g) candied peel, finely chopped	1 cupful candied peel, finely chopped
2 oz (50g) dried figs, finely chopped	½ cupful dried figs, finely chopped
1 oz (25g) carob powder	¼ cupful carob powder
2 oz (50g) plain wholemeal flour	½ cupful plain wholewheat flour
¼ teaspoonful ground cinnamon	¼ teaspoonful ground cinnamon
¼ teaspoonful ground mixed spice	¼ teaspoonful ground mixed spice
¼ teaspoonful ground mace	¼ teaspoonful ground mace
5 oz (150g) raw cane sugar	¾ cupful raw cane sugar
5 oz (150g) clear honey	½ cupful clear honey

1. Place the chopped nuts, candied peel, figs, carob powder, flour and spices in a mixing bowl and mix well.

2. Put the honey and sugar into a heavy-based saucepan; heat gently and stir until a teaspoonful of the syrup forms a soft ball when dropped into a cup of cold water or, if you have a sugar thermometer, until it reads 240°F (116°C).

3. Remove from the heat and stir in the fruit and nut mixture, and stir until well blended.

4. Press the mixture into a lined and greased 9 inch (23cm) loose-bottomed flan tin which is not less than 1½ inches (3cm) deep – the mixture should not come more than two-thirds up the side. Bake in a preheated cool oven 300°F/150°C (Gas Mark 2) for 30 minutes.

5. Turn out of the tin and allow to cool. Remove the greaseproof (wax) paper and transfer to a serving plate. Serve cut into wedges.

Note: Stored in an airtight tin, the *panforte* will keep for several weeks.

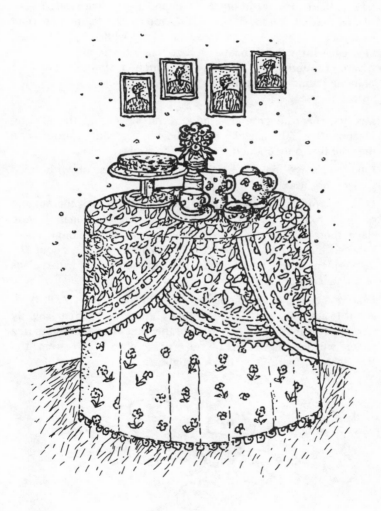

MACAROONS
Amaretti

(Makes about 24)

Imperial (Metric)	American
½ lb (225g) ground almonds	2 cupsful ground almonds
6 oz (175g) light Muscovado sugar	1 cupful light Muscovado sugar
3-4 drops natural almond essence	3-4 drops natural almond extract
1 to 1½ egg whites, lightly beaten	1 to 1½ egg whites, lightly beaten
Rice paper (optional)	Rice paper (optional)
12 blanched almonds, cut into strips	12 blanched almonds, cut into strips

1. Mix together the ground almonds, the sugar and the almond essence. Gradually add the lightly beaten egg whites, a little at a time, adding only enough to make a firm paste.

2. Line two large baking sheets with rice paper or with oiled greaseproof (wax) paper.

3. Dampen your hands and roll heaped teaspoonsful of the mixture between your palms to form biscuits the size of a small walnut. Place them on the prepared baking sheets with enough space between them to allow them to spread as they cook – about 1½ inches (4cm) and flatten them a little. Top each biscuit with a piece of blanched almond.

4. Bake in a preheated moderate oven, 350°F/180°F (Gas Mark 4) for about 15 minutes, until golden – they should have a crisp, slightly crunchy texture. Leave them to cool then cut away the excess rice paper surrounding each biscuit (or remove them from the greaseproof paper). Store in an airtight tin.

ITALIAN FRUIT SALAD
Macedonia di frutta

(Serves 4 to 6)

Imperial (Metric)	American
½ pint (275ml) freshly squeezed orange juice	1⅓ cupsful freshly squeezed orange juice
Juice and rind of ½ lemon	Juice and rind of ½ lemon
2 apples	2 apples
2 pears	2 pears
½ lb (225g) green or black grapes	2 cupsful green or black grapes
2 ripe peaches, when in season	2 ripe peaches, when in season
2 bananas	2 bananas
Clear honey, to taste	Clear honey, to taste
3 tablespoonsful orange liqueur (optional)	2 tablespoonsful orange liqueur (optional)

1. In a large bowl put the orange juice, the grated lemon rind and the lemon juice. Add each fruit to the bowl as you cut it, so that the juice in the bowl will keep it from discolouring.

2. Wash and cut apples and pears into quarters, but leave the peel on. Remove the cores and roughly chop into ½ inch (1 cm) cubes.

3. Wash the grapes and detach them from the clusters. Cut each one in half and remove the pips. Add seedless grapes whole to the bowl.

4. If using peaches, peel and cut into halves and remove the stones. Slice the peaches into the bowl.

5. Peel and slice the bananas straight into the bowl.

6. When all the fruit is in, add honey to taste and the optional orange liqueur. Toss lightly but well. Cover the bowl with cling film and chill in the refrigerator for at least 2 hours before serving.

PEARS IN RED WINE
Pere al vino

(Serves 4 to 6)

Imperial (Metric)	American
4-6 dessert pears	4-6 dessert pears
½ pint (275ml) red wine	1⅓ cupsful red wine
½ pint (275ml) water	1⅓ cupsful water
2-3 strips lemon rind, yellow part only	2-3 strips lemon rind, yellow part only
3 tablespoonsful raw cane sugar or honey	3 tablespoonsful raw cane sugar or honey
1 cinnamon stick	1 cinnamon stick

1. Peel the pears, leaving them whole and with the stalks still attached.

2. In a medium-sized saucepan, put the wine, water, lemon rind, sugar or honey, cinnamon stick and bring to the boil.

3. Put the pears into the pan, submerging them as much as possible in the wine mixture. Cover the pan and poach gently for 10-15 minutes, or until pears are tender when pierced with a knife. Do not overcook; they must hold their shape.

4. Carefully lift out the pears and put them into individual serving bowls.

5. Rapidly boil down the syrup. Taste and add more sweetener if needed. Pour the wine sauce over the pears. Serve at room temperature or cold.

Variations: Use other fruits, such as peaches, nectarines or apricots.

SUMMER FRUIT CUP
Cope misto bosco

(Serves 4)

Imperial (Metric)	American
1½ lbs (675g) mixed soft summer fruits: strawberries, raspberries, blackberries, etc.	1½ pounds mixed soft summer fruits: strawberries, raspberries, blackberries, etc.
¼ pint (150ml) medium-dry white wine or juice of 1 lemon	⅔ cupful medium-dry white wine or juice of 1 lemon
Clear honey, to taste	Clear honey, to taste

1. Put the washed and hulled fruit into a serving bowl. Cut large strawberries into halves.

2. Pour in the white wine or lemon juice and toss lightly to mix. Add honey to taste.

3. Chill for at least 1 hour before serving.

Note: The word *bosco* means woodland. In Italy this dish is made with tiny wild strawberries, wild raspberries and blackberries (from which it gets its name) which have flavours that cannot be matched by garden varieties.

ZABAGLIONE
Zabaione

(Serves 4 to 6)

Zabaione is probably one of the best-known Italian sweets.

Imperial (Metric)	American
4 egg yolks, large	4 egg yolks, large
2oz (50g) raw Muscovado sugar	⅓ cupful raw Muscovado sugar
¼ pint (150ml) Marsala (sweet sherry may be substituted)	⅔ cupful Marsala (sweet sherry may be substituted)

1. Put the egg yolks and the sugar into a heatproof glass bowl. Make sure you choose a large enough bowl as the mixture increases greatly in volume as you whisk it. Whisk with either a hand or electric whisk until the mixture becomes pale and fluffy.

2. Place the bowl over a saucepan of simmering water. Gradually add the Marsala and continue whisking. Do not on any account let the mixture boil, or let the bottom of the bowl touch the water. If the *zabaione* is cooked over direct heat it is very liable to curdle. The *zabaione* is ready when the mixture forms a dense foamy mass and holds its shape when you lift up the whisk. This process may take as long as 10 minutes.

3. Spoon the *zabaione* into large, stemmed glasses, and serve while it is still hot.

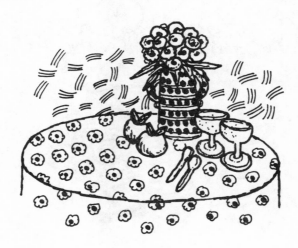

ALMOND STUFFED PEACHES
Pesche ripiene alla Piemontese

(Serves 6)

Imperial (Metric)	American
6 large firm but ripe peaches	6 large firm but ripe peaches
5-6 macaroons, crushed	5-6 macaroons, crushed
(see page 150)	(see page 150)
2 tablespoonsful honey	2 tablespoonsful honey
1½ oz (40g) butter	3 tablespoonsful butter
1 large egg yolk	1 large egg yolk

1. Halve the peaches without skinning them, and remove the stones. Scoop enough peach pulp out of each half to make a deep space in the centre. Add the pulp to the crushed macaroons, then stir in the honey, butter and egg yolk.

2. Stuff the peaches with the macaroon mixture, spreading it in a smooth mound over each half. Arrange the peach halves side by side in a buttered ovenproof dish.

3. Bake in a preheated moderate oven, 350°F/180°C (Gas Mark 4) for 25-30 minutes, until they are just tender. Serve warm or cold.

FIG TEA RING
Ciambella di fichi all'antica

(Makes 1 large ring approx. 12 inches/30 cm across)

For the dough:

Imperial (Metric)	American
⅓ pint (200 ml) milk	¾ cupful milk
1 oz (25 g) butter or polyunsaturated margarine	2½ tablespoonsful butter or polyunsaturated margarine
2 teaspoonsful honey	2 teaspoonsful honey
½ oz (15 g) fresh yeast or ¼ oz (7 g) dried yeast	1 tablespoonful fresh yeast or ½ tablespoonful dried yeast
¾ lb (350 g) wholemeal flour	3 cupsful wholewheat flour
½ teaspoonful sea salt	½ teaspoonful sea salt
1 egg	1 egg

For the filling:

Imperial (Metric)	American
1 lb (450 g) dried figs, chopped	3 cupsful chopped dried figs
4 oz (100 g) almonds, coarsely chopped	¾ cupful coarsely chopped almonds
½ teaspoonful ground cinnamon	½ teaspoonful ground cinnamon
2 tablespoonsful honey	2 tablespoonsful honey
Grated rind and juice of 1 orange	Grated rind and juice of 1 orange
4 tablespoonsful red wine	4 tablespoonsful red wine

1. Scald the milk and add the butter and margarine and honey. Stir until most of the butter melts. Cool to lukewarm, add the yeast and mix well. Leave in a warm place for 10 minutes to froth.

2. Place the flour into a warm bowl with the salt. Make a well in the centre, and pour in the yeast and milk mixture. Add the egg. Mix to a soft dough, adding more flour if necessary. Turn out onto a lightly floured surface and knead until smooth. Roll the dough into a 14 × 12 inches (35 × 30 cm) rectangle and set aside.

3. Place the chopped figs, almonds, cinnamon, honey, the orange rind and juice and the wine into a saucepan and simmer gently until thick. Cool.

4. Spread the filling evenly over the dough. Roll dough up fairly tightly like a Swiss-roll, brush the ends with water and join them to form a

circle. Leave, covered in a warm place, until doubled in size (about 45 minutes).

5. With a sharp knife or scissors, make deep cuts almost through the ring at intervals of 1 inch (2.5cm) twisting each segment at an angle. Place the ring on a greased baking tray. Bake in a preheated oven 375°F/190°C (Gas Mark 5) for 30-45 minutes.

SWEET EGG PASTRY
Pasta frolla

Imperial (Metric)	American
½ lb (225g) plain wholemeal flour	2 cupsful plain wholewheat flour
4 oz (100g) butter or	½ cupful butter or
polyunsaturated margarine –	polyunsaturated margarine –
at room temperature	at room temperature
2 egg yolks	2 egg yolks
1 oz (25g) raw cane sugar	2½ tablespoonsful raw cane
½ teaspoonful grated lemon rind	sugar
Pinch of sea salt	½ teaspoonful grated lemon rind
	Pinch of sea salt

1. Put the flour into a large mixing bowl. Add the margarine or butter and cut it into small pieces. Rub the fat into the flour with your fingertips or a fork, whichever is easiest, until the mixture resembles fine breadcrumbs.

2. Make a well in the centre and put in the egg yolks, sugar, lemon rind and salt. Add 1 or 2 tablespoonsful of ice cold water and mix the ingredients until they form a firm dough. It should just hold together and be pliable, but not be damp and sticky. Do not knead the dough or work it any more than is necessary.

3. Roughly shape it into a ball. Wrap the dough in greaseproof (wax) paper or film wrap and put it in the refrigerator and chill for at least 1 hour – this will greatly improve the pastry. Use as required.

Index